Supercharge Your Mana
Role

Making the transition to internal consultant

To Jan, Ben and Hannah for their patience.

Mark

To Christine, for all your support, to my parents for all your guidance and to Matt and Tarek for being my brothers.

Sam

Supercharge Your Management Role

Making the transition to internal consultant

Mark Thomas and Sam Elbeik

Butterworth-Heinemann
Linacre House, Jordan Hill, Oxford OX2 8DP
A division of Reed Educational and Professional Publishing Ltd

ℛ A member of the Reed Elsevier plc group

OXFORD   BOSTON   JOHANNESBURG
MELBOURNE   NEW DELHI   SINGAPORE

First published 1996

British Library Cataloguing in Publication Data
Mark Thomas
    Supercharge your management role: making the transition to
    internal consultant
    1   Management   2   Business consultants
    I   Title II. Elbeik, Sam
    658.4'6

ISBN 0 7506 2546 5

Typeset by Datix International Limited, Bungay, Suffolk
Printed in Great Britain by Clays Ltd, St Ives plc

Contents

Mark Thomas
Director, Performance Dynamics
Mark Thomas is a Director of Performance Dynamics, an international consultancy specializing in organization development and transformation. He has extensive industrial, commercial and consulting experience covering major change scenarios involving organization restructuring, mergers and acquisitions and strategic reviews. In addition to his consulting work he runs a range of executive development programmes throughout Europe, SE Asia and Australasia. Mark was educated at the University of Wales and the London School of Economics and is a Fellow of the Institute of Personnel and Development in the UK.

Sam Elbeik
Director, Performance Dynamics and IT Centre Limited
Dr Sam Elbeik has over fifteen years' experience in information technology. He specializes in providing project management training and IT consultancy support to the corporate environment as well as delivering rapidly developed information and financial systems, largely for the banking and human resource sector. He has a BSc(Hons) in Management and Chemistry and a PhD in Electrochemistry from The City University, London. He is an active committee member of the British Computer Society and technical reviewer for *Computing*.

Acknowledgements

We would like to thank the following people who kindly gave up their time to share their very real experiences and advice with us and others: Curt Blattner, Nestlé Group; Dalim Basu, Independent Television Network; Peter Brunner, Mercedes-Benz AG; Anisa Caine, Peak Potential; Lewis Doyle, Legal and General; Tony Edgar, Lloyds Bank; Peter Fraser, Zurich Australian Insurance; Mike Gelder, Lloyds Bank; Alan Goodson, Dow Chemicals; Marcia Hershkovitz, Novo Nordisk; Robin Lanman, Mayne Nickless Courier Systems; Enid Murphy, Telstra, Australia; David Ohlmüs, Department of Immigration and Ethnic Affairs, Australia; Peter Stewart, Power-Gen UK.

We are grateful to Data General for allowing us to use one of their advertisements.

A special thanks to Alf Chattell, Ernst and Young, who provided expertise and guidance on our process mapping section.

1 Essentials of internal consultancy

WHY INTERNAL CONSULTANCY?

We titled this book *Supercharge Your Management Role* to reflect the radical changes taking place in managerial roles and support functions in today's organizations. The accelerating spread and transfer of knowledge and technology to all parts of the globe has created a highly competitive and volatile economic environment. Organizations must now move faster than ever before in order to compete and prosper. To achieve this capability, organization structures and job roles must be flexible and responsive. Old methods of organizing will no longer provide tomorrow's growth. Existing concepts of management which rely heavily on notions of planning, checking, co-ordinating and approving people's actions are currently the subject of intensive review.

The classic managerial role of command and control that has traditionally characterized organizations is fast becoming obsolete. The old management maxim of 'do as I say because I am the boss' is crumbling if not already dead. Many of the roles now being performed in today's leading organizations demand people who are highly educated, skilled and motivated. The notion that power and reward in an organization should be based on position and status is giving way to the notion of individual 'worth and contribution'. At the same time, age-old commitments to areas of functional expertise such as finance, human resources, marketing and production are in decline. Organizations are rapidly moving towards organizing around processes and outcomes. This approach removes complexity from an organization by replacing traditional functional barriers and boundaries with a new and sharper focus on the power of simplicity.

These radical shifts mean that new models of managing organizations are being sought for the late 1990s and beyond. One clear fact is that we are not going to need the numbers of managers we have required in the past. For those managers who will be required, the demand will be that they operate very differently than in the past. In the future, management will not control, but will provide the conditions and support that enable highly skilled and knowledgeable people to perform at their maximum capability. The key word here is leverage – the ability of an organization to maximize its people capability without the need for excessive and expensive management controls. The manager who has traditionally relied on positional authority to achieve results will become a thing of the past. Winning organizations will seek to develop and promote a concept of managing that is about putting people at the centre of competitive advantage.

SHIFTING THE CONSULTING FOCUS

Many of you will be familiar with the problems and disasters associated with external consultants who have entered organizations, displaying huge amounts of arrogance, who, all too frequently, believed they knew what the problem was, even before asking any questions. This form of behaviour characterizes the worst form of consulting and frequently results in an enormous waste of time, effort and resources. The classic story of the external consultant who borrows your watch to tell you the time, charges you for it and then keeps the watch is perhaps a little exaggerated, but reality seems to suggest a lot of evidence for the caricature. Of course, there will always be good and bad external consultants. It also seems likely that there will always be opportunities for good external consultants to thrive. But so often the solution to a problem already exists in an organization before the arrival of an external consultant.

Many of you will also have had direct experience of,

or recognize, organizations which are too flawed in the way they are managed to listen to their own people when it comes to diagnosing problems and developing solutions. People inside organizations know what the problems are, they understand the issues and have the ideas to fix them, but so often their views and ideas are either ignored or dismissed. One of the central themes of this book is to challenge this depressing convention and help you grasp what is a major opportunity to enhance your organization's performance as well as your own.

It is against this complex background of radical change that we believe the model of internal consultancy has much to offer today's organization. Internal consultancy provides an exciting framework to help today's manager deal with many of the challenges. Internal consultancy is an operating style which aligns itself to the demands of flatter organizational structures and highly skilled and knowledgeable workers. Internal consultancy harnesses the expertise and experience of the traditional manager without the negative behaviours of petty political squabbles, in-fighting and posturing which have so often defined management behaviour. Figure 1.1 illustrates the mindset differences between the internal consultant and the traditional manager.

Internal consultancy promotes the concept of enabling people to develop solutions to their own organizational problems and, in so doing, develop their long-term capability as well as that of their organization. Internal consultancy really does provide a basis for managers to supercharge their existing roles into the future.

HOW TO USE THIS BOOK

This book will provide you with a detailed and practical understanding of the skills involved in becoming an internal consultant. Many of the individual skills outlined may not be new to you – indeed, it is likely that you may well have already completed some form of

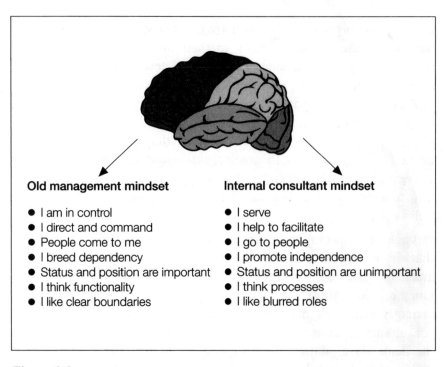

Old management mindset

- I am in control
- I direct and command
- People come to me
- I breed dependency
- Status and position are important
- I think functionality
- I like clear boundaries

Internal consultant mindset

- I serve
- I help to facilitate
- I go to people
- I promote independence
- Status and position are unimportant
- I think processes
- I like blurred roles

Figure 1.1

presentation or report writing skills training. But internal consultancy brings together an array of skills in a concentrated manner and then combines them with a distinctive client perspective and focus. You can successfully develop these skills through practice and experience and, in so doing, dramatically enhance your capability and worth.

We believe that the role of internal consultant is now assuming greater importance within organizations and is expanding beyond the esoteric areas of organizational development which characterized earlier efforts to establish a consultancy base. We see internal consultancy and its associated skills breaking into the mainstream of organizational life and in particular the role of line managers and support functions. The internal consultancy model offers immense benefits in harnessing and actively promoting internal knowledge and expertise to improve organizational performance. The potential prize and goal is a style of managing that is in tune with the fluid and ever-changing nature of today's organization.

We will explain the stages involved in operating as a successful internal consultant and detail the actions involved in managing client relationships and projects. We will also address the challenges involved in making the transition from line manager to internal consultant. Should you simply want to harness some of the operating style of internal consultancy to enhance your existing organizational role, you will find much to meet your needs as the skills and practices detailed in this book are generic. Indeed, they can be applied to almost any management role in some capacity or other.

We have written this book with a strong emphasis on the practical 'How to' aspects of internal consultancy. We have not set out to teach you anything about your technical or functional areas of expertise, be it information technology, finance, total quality or human resources. It will, however, provide you with a process to manage your clients and projects in a professional and successful manner. We have included many checklists and templates to assist you. We firmly believe that these skills represent the start of a new business order and that in the future organizations will increasingly look to managers to 'consult' rather than manage.

THE CHANGING NATURE OF ORGANIZATIONS AND MANAGEMENT

We live in a world of accelerating change where the future is more uncertain than ever. Every day, organizations are announcing major shifts in strategies, product lines, service offerings and people. Technology is promoting new forms of organization structure and location is becoming less of an issue as regards where work is organized and executed. Our old assumptions about how to design, manage and run organizations are now the subject of radical review. The fact is that we are involved in a period of major transition, where simply doing more of what we have done in the past will not sustain us in the future. Today we have to manage by the 'second hand' not the calendar. Increasingly the question is not, Are we better this year than last year?, but, Are we better today than we were yesterday? Organizations are looking to develop new capabilities of speed, innovation and flexibility.

As organizations pursue the benefits of rapid technological development and power, so too are new ideas and notions about managing people being explored and applied. Concepts such as empowerment and self-managed teams seek to place greater emphasis on people accepting increased responsibility and control for their work. Such ideas are gaining ground throughout the competitive world. As a result, it is becoming clear that what managers have traditionally practised is being questioned. In many organizations the classic planning, directing, controlling and reviewing functions of management are being transferred to people who carry out the work at the point of execution. The race to do it 'right first time' means that organizations can no longer afford large numbers of managers controlling or checking people. Self-management is rapidly becoming the philosophy and approach that many organizations wish to operate.

It is important to recognize that this fundamental change is not born out of some sense of well-being towards people. Indeed, the number of organizations that pursue these concepts from a sense of real vision and belief in the power of people capability as a competitive weapon are still few. No, the real driving forces for most organizations are cost-competitive pressures. Many middle management roles are simply too cumbersome and expensive for organizations to compete against faster and more innovative low-cost competitors. The result is a desire to explore new and more radical approaches to the notion of supervision as a means of reducing costs and accelerating competitive capabilities. Many of our existing organizational concepts and practices have their roots in the 1950s genre of management, so real innovation has been a long time in coming.

'The bigger my budget and head count, the bigger fish I am' philosophy has historically been the basis on which many successful management careers have been built. Indeed, such behaviours have been actively encouraged by many organizational reward and appraisal systems. For example, traditional job evaluation techniques have often rewarded jobs that have been characterized by size in terms of the numbers of staff reporting and budget responsibility. But these types of approach have often resulted in management behaviours and practices consisting of internal politicking, empire building and game playing – none of which add value or service to the customer. It is also an approach which results in people becoming overly reliant on their managers to make decisions and take action. In many of today's leading organizations this traditional form of management activity is viewed as reactive. Organizations which possess and promote dependency cultures will not win in today's information- and knowledge-based era.

In order that organizations can become more innovative, flexible and customer-responsive, they need to devolve power to the point of customer contact. This requires people to be highly trained and also empowered to take decisions which were previously in the exclusive realm of managers. Thus we enter a new world of organizational working, where self-directed teams rely on their collective motivation, skills and capabilities to get things done. Rather like the Formula One racing pit team, when it comes to the real work you neither need nor want someone hovering over your shoulder to tell you whether you have done it right or not. The reality is that you know it already; at the same time your, commitment and skills ensure that for 99.9 per cent of the time you are delivering! Consequently, management in the traditional sense becomes an irrelevance. Figure 1.2 shows the differences between the old and the new organization.

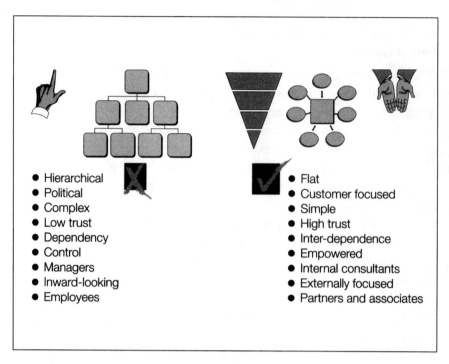

- Hierarchical
- Political
- Complex
- Low trust
- Dependency
- Control
- Managers
- Inward-looking
- Employees

- Flat
- Customer focused
- Simple
- High trust
- Inter-dependence
- Empowered
- Internal consultants
- Externally focused
- Partners and associates

Figure 1.2 *Organizations are changing structures and demanding more flexibility*

We are therefore at the beginning of a major shift in the world of work – a shift which is already having immense implications in terms of how we think about organizations and how they need to be designed and managed. These changes will, however, continue to bring pain, as organizations continue to pursue major reductions in the numbers of people they employ. Many people no longer derive satisfaction from their work. Indeed, we see managers arriving at their offices and feeling under siege from a 'more and more with less and less' approach. Managers are desperately looking for motivation and security in a hostile corporate environment. Given the radical shifts taking place, there is little doubt that managers will continue to face immense pressures to re-assess their roles, increase productivity and demonstrate real added value. Faced with these challenges, we believe that the internal consulting model provides an attractive role for managers to adopt. It has the capability to provide managers with a means to move towards a more focused role in the knowledge era.

SUPPORT FUNCTIONS UNDER ATTACK

Another aspect of these dramatic changes is that traditional organizational support functions are also under review. Concepts such as business process re-engineering, with its emphasis on eradicating non-value added activities, have resulted in many critical appraisals of conventional support functions such as human resources, finance, internal audit and information technology. Many of these functions are now having to make significant changes to their methods of operation. Faced with competitive pressures, organizations are no longer prepared to fund activities which neither add real value to the organization, nor support the provision of quality or service to the customer. Figure 1.3

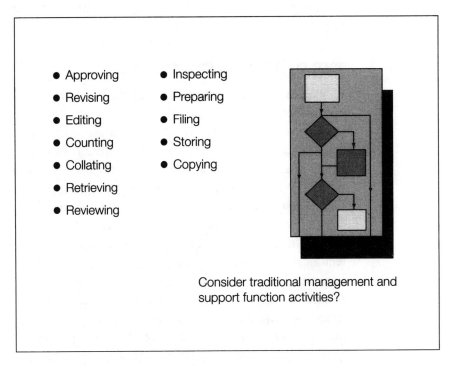

- Approving
- Revising
- Editing
- Counting
- Collating
- Retrieving
- Reviewing
- Inspecting
- Preparing
- Filing
- Storing
- Copying

Consider traditional management and support function activities?

Figure 1.3   *Does the process add value, service to the customer or cost?*

highlights the kinds of non-value added activities that can be identified in many traditional support functions and, for that matter, management roles.

When subjected to rigorous analysis and the question 'Why do we do that?', it becomes clear that many aspects of the work of the traditional support function add little to the central nature of the organization. All too often, support functions have developed to the stage where they consume large amounts of resources without necessarily contributing to the organization's fundamental goals. In many ways they can be said to have replicated the worst aspects of the old managerial model of controlling and checking and, as such, face similar challenges in terms of refocusing their role and contribution. The temptation for any support function is to turn inwards and see itself as the primary customer in organizational relationships. Thus it loses sight of its central aim and purpose and begins to become an end in itself, often growing excessively and engaging in blocking rather than supporting activities to the organization.

THE OPPORTUNITY AWAITS

It is against all these fundamental shifts in the world of work and organizations that we have observed the increasing development and use of internal consultants. Internal consultants achieve results through influence rather than the direct application of formal executive power. While being aware of the inherent political nature of organizations, internal consultants avoid becoming involved in complex and negative inter-departmental rivalry or politics. By using their specialist technical knowledge, influencing skills and models of organizational change, internal consultants achieve performance improvements. Their method of operating is to enable people to solve organizational problems without the classic need to claim credit for success which for so long has been the driving force for much managerial behaviour. On a strategic level, we see internal consultancy providing the following benefits:

- A more flexible and responsive organizational role for managers which is based on contribution, not status; and, as such, is in tune with the future direction of winning organizations
- An overwhelming focus on managers demonstrating 'value added' services or contributions to their organizations as opposed to controlling, interfering and posturing-type contributions
- A new people management relationship which is based on a consultant–client concept rather than a command and control regime
- A move to a process-based organization with the resulting removal of traditional loyalties to functional areas of expertise and disciplines and, with that, the traditional hostilities.

The emphasis that internal consultancy places on moving from a *'colleague to a client'* working relationship can bring major new benefits to both managers and support functions that have always, and without question, been supported by their organization. Indeed, the very essence of a client-centred consulting relationship involves providing a level of service that easily exceeds the controlling and bureaucratic tendencies of many managers and traditional support functions. As such, the model has particular relevance to the following organizational roles:

- Information technology and systems specialists
- Finance and internal audit professionals
- Human resources or personnel specialists
- Training and development specialists
- Business development specialists
- Project managers
- Administration managers
- Facilities management
- Customer service and support specialists
- Total quality management specialists.

All these roles have to provide quality advice and services to their organization. If managing and supporting roles are to thrive and prosper in the future, then the people occupying them will need to focus on providing value added services. Already many organizations have outsourced management and support function activities, with the result that internal customers have the choice to buy external resources. This trend has accelerated in the areas of information technology, human resources, training and development and facilities management. As a result, competition is becoming a daily reality for many internal support functions. The internal consultancy model offers a positive response to these challenges. The emphasis it places on understanding clients' needs and delivering high value added services can bring immense benefits for managers and support functions that have lost focus on their roles and contributions.

WHAT IS CONSULTANCY?

To understand the internal consultancy role we must first define the nature of consultancy work so as to differentiate it from more conventional forms of management. A consultant's work begins when part of an organization's structure, processes or systems are failing to deliver the necessary levels of performance. Consultants are employed to improve the performance gap and their contribution might involve a total solution or the provision of some form of specialist technical support for an agreed period of time. To that extent, their involvement in a project can be of a short-term or long-term nature. The consultant's role is to assist the client without taking over control of the problem. Good consultancy is also about providing advice in such a way that it enhances the client's ability to solve their future problems and challenges. The consultant, in effect, leaves something behind – an improved capability. This is why we believe the role has so much potential for managers operating in flatter structures with empowered workforces.

Much of a consultant's work also involves the management of change. While having to influence a client and a situation to get things done differently, you must achieve this so that the client becomes fully committed to the solution. Being able to influence your clients without any formal executive power is one of the defining characteristics of the role. Successful consultants do not rely on overt authority or control to succeed – instead, they rely on their high levels of expertise and influencing skills to persuade people to move to action.

THE DIFFERENCE BETWEEN EXPERT AND PROCESS CONSULTING

There are two quite distinct types of consulting style, involving the expert and the process consultant. Both have very different characteristics and methods of working with clients. Figure 1.4 highlights some of the characteristics and advantages and disadvantages of

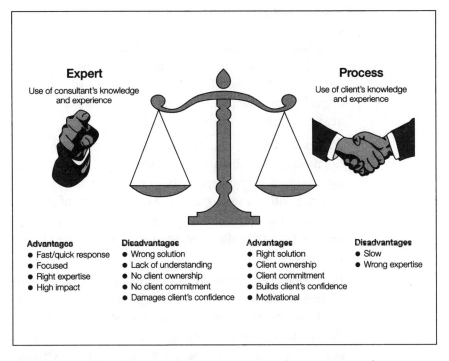

Figure 1.4 *The difference between expert and process consultancy*

both types. Most of you will be familiar with expert consulting, which is typified by the classic external consultant who applies all his or her knowledge and expertise to diagnose and solve the client's problem in a directive and often prescriptive manner. This form of consulting is very attractive to clients as it can be applied in a very fast and focused way. Information technology, for example, has traditionally been an area which has been dominated by expert consulting.

The major difficulty with expert consulting is the lack of client ownership or commitment that results. All too often, the recommendations of expert consultants falter at the implementation stage because insufficient emphasis has been placed on establishing and developing the client's commitment to the outcomes of the consultant's work. Expert consulting involves a directive style and, while it is very fast, it does mean that significant issues like client involvement and ownership can be overlooked.

Expert consulting can also prove ineffective in developing the long-term capability of clients. When expert consultants complete their work they often take their expertise away with them, so that the client is unable to cope with similar problems in the future. Expert consulting can therefore have the effect of breeding organizational dependency on the consultant. Clients are unable to operate without the expertise.

The excessive use of expert consultancy can also lower the morale of a client's organization as it assumes that the knowledge and capability to deal with the problem was not within the scope of the client's team of people. This can be very demotivating, particularly if people believe that they do have the capability to tackle the problem.

In its defence, expert consulting does have the benefit of being able to address the right problem with the right expertise. An organization cannot always be sure that it does have the necessary solution to a problem, and so there may well be a need to bring in expertise in very specialist fields to tackle challenging issues. To that extent, expert consulting will always have a place in organizations and so remain a credible approach, despite its limitations.

An example of expert and process consulting

A definition of highly available computing – The expert consultant

'The use of redundant components in conjunction with appropriate fall-over and restart mechanisms in both hardware and software to permit event notification of failure conditions coupled with application and/or database checkpointing and rollback/recover algorithms, thus establishing reasonable assurance within predicted norms that a combination of redundancies will allow a confidence factor to exist and that mean time to repair shall be a small enough variable in conjunction with simultaneous mean time between failure of the aforementioned redundant components that the overall system availability will be significantly above normal performance.'

Commonsense translation – The process consultant

'Your computer system should be up and running 24 hours a day, 7 days a week, 365 days a year, so you don't have to be.'

Adapted from an advertisement placed by Data General, Economist, *November 1994*

Courtesy of Data General

In contrast, process consulting works on the assumption that a client has the necessary capability to address the problem, but needs guidance and advice in the 'how to' element of addressing the problem. The emphasis is therefore on helping a client to think through the problem and produce a solution which has a very high degree of commitment and ownership. The major difficulty with process consulting is that it can be much more time-consuming than the expert approach. Developing commitment through involvement and discussion is always a longer process, and frequently the urgency of organizational life prevents such time being expended on problem solving. Quick-fix solutions are so often the order of the day.

Process consulting also works on the assumption that your client has the necessary expertise to tackle the problem. This, of course, may not be true. So you may end up wasting a lot of time addressing a problem with the wrong approach, whereas the prompt application of some form of expert consulting would have remedied the situation.

Conversely, when it works well, process consulting has the added benefit of enhancing a client's ability to deal with the problem the next time it happens. As such, it improves the organization's overall capability, which is something that cannot always be said for expert consulting.

When selecting forms of consulting, organizations frequently choose the expert approach because it appears to offer greater benefits in terms of speed and focus. In practice, these benefits prove more imaginary than real, and much of this book will focus on the process skills that you may need to accompany your underlying technical expertise. By combining both sets of skills we believe that people can develop into truly outstanding internal consultants.

'A consultant is like a tightrope walker; to master the job you must be focused, aware and balanced at all times. At one end of the tightrope you are a counsellor, at the other end an expert; the skill is to know where you should be at any particular moment.'

Anisa Caine
Personal Development
Consultant
Peak Potential

Depending on your functional area of expertise, most internal consultants will need to develop an agility to balance themselves on the expert and process continuum (Figure 1.5). Knowing where to be on this continuum at any one time is the art of a good consultant. All too often, external consultants totally under-estimate the power of process management in developing their client's capability and generating commitment to and ownership of solutions. Hence our general ability to recall horror stories involving external consultants who didn't listen and simply imposed solutions. As an internal consultant, while you will apply your technical expertise – whether it be in the areas of project management, systems design, training

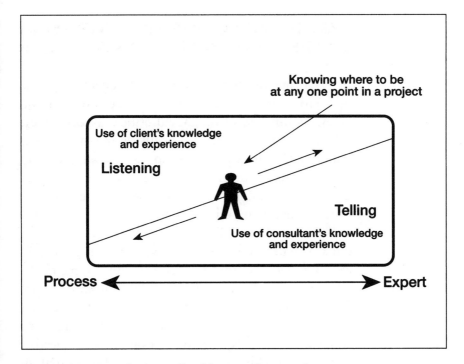

Figure 1.5 *Developing a flexible consulting style*

or financial planning – you must recognize the potential dangers of assuming that, as the expert, you know all the answers, thus forcing your solution onto your client regardless of their views. Process consulting demands that you focus not only on the problem but also on the client.

The reality of most organizational problems is that there is never one right answer to solve a problem, there are several. Consequently, success in consulting terms involves getting to one of those solutions. But more important than that is getting your client to the solution that they are most committed to and feel most comfortable with. If you do this, you are likely to gain immense credibility with your client. Recognizing when you need to challenge your clients and when you need to step back are key skills that you will need to develop. So your ability to balance the expert and process scale is key to your success as a skilled internal consultant.

THE DIFFERENCE BETWEEN INTERNAL AND EXTERNAL CONSULTANTS

In exploring the nature of internal consultancy it is useful to begin with a comparison with external consultancy, as this helps to highlight critical aspects of the role. In examining differences between the two it is not our intention to set one group against another, but simply to recognize that there are key differences and that they can influence selection decisions concerning which route your clients will take. As an internal consultant, these differences should influence your thinking when you come to actively market your services. You will see from the list below that some of the differences can be used aggressively to promote a case for using internal consultancy as opposed to adopting the external route. At the same time, there are some issues which will require you to examine and question your own ability to be objective and impartial in carrying out internal projects.

In some situations you may well find yourself competing with external consultants for an internal project. You therefore need to have a clear view of the relative advantages and disadvantages of either approach in order to shape your business case and proposals.

External consultants are:

- employed for a fixed period to work on a specific client problem

- potentially able to get the full attention of senior managers more easily – clients tend to value more what they have to pay for

- presented as experts – they have specialist expertise and experience which is not present in the organization. This is often combined with an extensive knowledge of either specific or different industries which clients find very attractive

- generally highly motivated and committed people who display high levels of energy towards their work and their clients. While many are paid lots of money for doing this, their motivation and commitment is often to their work and clients first and their pay cheque second

- not always conversant with their client's business. Thus the client may have to pay for the consultant to learn about the business in the initial stages of a project. This can be expensive

- a flexible resource. The organization is not burdened with long-term costs – when the work is finished the consultant leaves (although in some organizations this never seems to happen!)

- able to learn from their clients and use this learning with other clients

- not emotionally involved in their client's problems – they have no history of investment in the situation and can therefore be more objective and critical in reviewing situations

- independent – this is, of course, debatable

- often investing in new approaches and methodologies – they have to have something new to offer clients

- not always required to live with the consequences of their work

- not always being entirely honest when they say 'we've done this!' What they often mean is that 'we haven't, but we have really great people and expertise and we are really confident that we will find a solution'

- capable of developing a sense of dependency from their clients - 'we cannot function without you now'

- in a business themselves – they are selling people and time and are interested in consultant utilization and profit maximization.

Internal consultants are:

- employed full-time by the organization
- likely to understand the overall business better than external consultants
- sometimes more knowledgeable than external consultants. They should know their business and industry extremely well. They may also have developed an approach or methodology which is ahead of any external consultancy group
- normally part of a specific function (information technology, training and development, finance, business development)
- aware of the right language and culture of the organization. They know how things work and how to get things done
- able to identify with the organization and its ambitions – as employees they have a big emotional commitment
- liable to be taken for granted or lacking the credibility of some external consultants
- prone to being too emotionally involved in an organization – thus perhaps influencing their ability to be truly objective
- required to live with the consequences of their advice – they are still around long after the external consultants have left
- able to spread their knowledge and experience throughout the organization – they can enhance your organization's overall capability
- required to redefine past organizational relationships – the move from 'colleague' to 'client' requires a period of adjustment.

INSIGHT

Working with external consultants

In our experience, most external consultants are highly motivated and committed people who want to succeed and deliver high-quality work. However, because of the negative perception that people in organizations frequently have of external consultants, there can be a tendency for them to be hostile towards external consultants. This often results in difficult and strained relationships on joint projects.

If you work with external consultants on a project, seek to work with them and harness their skills and expertise rather than adopt a negative or antagonistic approach. Good external consultants will always respond to positive people and both sides will gain. So get closer. Don't distance yourself, see it as a learning opportunity – but at the same time make sure that your positive approach is reciprocated. Don't allow people simply to use you.

So if these are some of the essential differences between internal and external consultants, what about the more detailed aspects of the role?

Internal consultancy is an independent service

Many organizational problems occur because managers become too involved with a problem and so close their minds to certain possibilities or solutions. The need for fresh and independent thinking is one of the main reasons why external consultants are used so often, although, as we have already stated, it is arguable whether external consultants are truly independent. Someone, somewhere, is always paying the bill, and that can always influence what is reported or recommended. So the ability of internal consultants to provide an independent analysis of a situation is one of their most valued contributions. However, this is an extremely difficult role to play because as an internal consultant you are paid by your organization and, as such, part of it. Being critical of something to which you belong and which also ensures your financial well-being can be hazardous. You may also frequently need to challenge your client on difficult or contentious issues. This may involve confronting managers who are senior in status to you. In many organizations this

'For me the whole issue of successful internal consultancy is to regard yourself as being in for the long haul. There is no walking away from the fact – the decisions you make or are party to require you to live with the consequences for a long time – which is very different to the external consultant who is more like a tourist – someone who can spoil the environment and leave it for someone else to clean up.'

Peter Fraser
Group Human Resources
Consultant
Zurich Australian Insurance
Group

can be an extremely challenging task for anyone. Yet providing an independent perspective is an essential requirement of the role. Your clients frequently need to have their assumptions and methods questioned. Simply operating as a 'rubber stamp' and confirming a positive image on everything your client is doing may mean that you are failing to carry out an effective consulting role. The challenge of your client's objectives, aims and plans is part of your day-to-day role as an internal consultant.

Internal consultancy is an advisory service

Internal consultants are not employed to take difficult decisions on behalf of harassed or over-worked managers. As advisers, internal consultants are responsible for the quality and integrity of their advice, but it is their clients who ultimately bear the responsibility for implementation. Providing 'advice' in consulting terms can range from a technical input to the provision of counselling or facilitation expertise, but providing the right advice, in the right manner and at the right time is the critical skill of any effective consultant.

> 'As an internal consultant you are there to help your clients to be able to do things on their own and in a better way; your functioning is to support them. You should not allow yourself to get hooked into doing things for them or you will end up with all the tasks they don't want to do. Your role is that of a sparring partner and a coach not a slave!'
>
> *Marcia Hershkovitz*
> *Human Resource Specialist*
> *Novo Nordisk, Denmark*

For the line manager using the skills of the internal consultant, the objective is to empower his or her team to develop its own solution rather than impose one – the emphasis being on consulting and enabling, rather than directing and controlling.

Internal consultancy is the application of specialist knowledge, skills and experience

'Stay curious and sharp.'

Enid Murphy, Internal Consultant, Telstra Australia

Internal consultants are often employed to work on a problem when part of their organization is either short of specialist skills or lacks the necessary expertise. Depending on your technical background, your contribution may involve the introduction of new systems or operational methods. In other cases, the problem may be of a more general nature and involve you operating as a facilitator rather than a technical expert. As a facilitator, you are seeking to provide your client with a framework or process to help them solve the problem than rather provide a direct technical or expert input. We see the facilitator role as another change from the conventional line perspective which says, 'I will now take over!' Yes, as an internal consultant you have to provide advice and direction, but you must stop short of taking over the leadership mantle for the problem.

> 'You must be focused. As an internal consultant you have the advantage of knowing the system, but you must be aware of becoming trapped in your organization; unable to see the wood for the trees. Often your clients have lost their ability to focus on their problem and this lack of focus results in a scattering of energy.'
>
> *Anisa Caine*
> *Personal Development*
> *Consultant*
> *Peak Potential*

All internal consultants must ensure that their knowledge base and expertise is up-to-date. The ability to comment on or talk about the latest developments in your field of expertise or what is best practice in your industry gives you credibility and power with your clients. You have to work hard at developing your skills and knowledge base, as that is what your clients are ultimately buying. If all you can do as a consultant is talk about a very narrow and limited range of expertise and experience you will find it difficult to get clients to listen to you.

Internal consultancy is a proactive role

'Raise your profile by offering to contribute to projects.'
David Ohlmüs, Human Resource Consultant, Department of Immigration and Ethnic Affairs, Canberra

We have already identified the attraction of the internal consultant role to traditional support functions such as human resources and information technology. Moreover we are already seeing organizations making moves towards establishing such units. In our experience, simply changing the title of your department to Internal Consultancy Unit will not result in any immediate overnight transformation – indeed, if your organization has a negative perception of your department or support function you will need to work hard at changing this image. Simply sitting in your office and waiting for the telephone to ring might (depending on the previous performance of your department) mean waiting for a very long time. Internal consultancy demands a proactive approach with lots of positive networking throughout your organization. You will need to explore and identify problem areas and look for opportunities to assist your clients in tackling business challenges. You will also need to develop some kind of marketing plan either for yourself or for your group as part of this initiative. Our section on marketing will explore these issues in more depth, but being an internal consultant means that you have to start putting yourself around your organization.

Internal consultancy requires a higher business perspective

To become a highly successful internal consultant you will need to possess or develop an ability to contribute beyond any narrow areas of functional expertise. While traditional organizations have encouraged functional areas of expertise, we have all experienced the barriers and hostilities that spring up between functions and departments. Petty conflicts between sales and marketing, research and production are so common in organizations. Any internal consultant or unit, no matter what their area of expertise, must rise above feelings of professional or functional loyalty and display a higher and wider business perspective. Internal consultants must see themselves as business people first and functional experts second. To contribute truly to major business issues you need to be recognized within your organization as an informed person who understands the full business picture and not just a narrow range of technical issues. This again demands a strong sense of personal commitment and development to ensure that you keep up-to-date with external issues involving the economy, politics and competitor activity. Clients gain confidence from dealing with consultants they see as knowledgeable and

'Try to get on top of as many aspects of your business as you can and always keep your organization's strategy in mind. See the big picture.'

Peter Fraser
Group Human Resources
Consultant
Zurich Australian Insurance
Group

'Understand the key business drivers and the fixed and variable cost/ revenue implications for business areas concerned. Be clear as to how everything fits into the overall corporate jigsaw.'

Lewis Doyle
Business Development
Manager
Legal and General

well-informed. Narrow perspectives and outlooks do not impress, and if you want to get involved in major organizational issues you need to develop a well-rounded outlook on the world in which your organization operates. Be aware of your technical expertise and continually develop it, but do not allow it to become all-consuming.

Internal consultancy requires flexibility, personal confidence and credibility

'Don't empathise too much, working with superiors does not reduce the amount of challenge that you may need to do to achieve results.'

Peter Stewart, Business Development Manager, PowerGen UK

As you may be beginning to realize, internal consultancy is a challenging and demanding role. On one level it can involve a very clear and explicit role, but on another it has the potential to be ambiguous, with lots of changing priorities and no clearly defined set of day-to-day tasks. Consequently, as an internal consultant you will need to be comfortable with a 'loose' role which may involve not knowing what you are going to be doing from one day to another. For some people, this can provoke a sense of discomfort, as they prefer a job which involves a clearly defined set of tasks and responsibilities. But this is not what internal consultancy involves. To operate successfully, you have to be comfortable with ambiguous situations, and at the same time, display a high degree of self-confidence and credibility.

You must also feel at ease when working with different groups, including your senior colleagues, and be prepared to challenge and confront them on important issues. You need to be able to do this without appearing rude, arrogant or patronizing. Ultimately, your influence and power can only come from the quality of your advice and the manner in which you deliver it. It is not a role for the faint-hearted or introverted!

SO WHY USE AN INTERNAL CONSULTANT?

In the following section we examine the reasons for employing internal consultants on a project or assignment. We will be working on the assumption that your organization has the capability to establish a consulting unit and that this unit might evolve or develop out of an existing specialist support function role or a more general business development group. Alternatively, if you are going to be operating on an individual basis you might want to reflect on the reasons why you are being hired as you get involved in projects and other types of internal client work.

'I believe it is important to understand the reasons why you are going to be used and assess the chances of success. An external consultant can walk away and still work elsewhere "unmarked". If an internal consultant's credibility has suffered everyone else in the organisation knows.'

Peter Stewart
Business Development Manager
PowerGen UK

Internal consultants can be used for many different reasons, so it is important to understand the circumstances surrounding a project or assignment and to establish why you are being asked to provide assistance. Understanding your client's motives at an early stage can offset problems later on in your client relationship. Your client's motives for employing you can either be positive or negative, and in some situations you may have to deal with both. Listed below are some of the classic reasons for using consultants. You will need to look out in particular for the negatives, as they can be hazardous to your success.

Positive uses of consultants

To improve organizational efficiency

Improving organizational efficiency is perhaps the most obvious and common reason for using consultants. Organization structure and efficiency reviews involving overhead cost reductions are classic consultancy projects, as are those involved with improving operational performance through new management information systems. More recently, we have seen the widespread use of business process reviews, which involve mapping organizational processes in order to streamline core organizational processes. In other situations there may be problems involving customer response times or quality control problems which necessitate a multi-functional response involving systems and training and development expertise. In all these projects the objective in using consultants is to apply an independent and expert perspective and resource on a difficult and urgent problem.

Supplying an intensive and focused resource on a temporary basis

Major organizational change involving a re-organization or the development of a management information system requires large amounts of senior management time. Day-to-day operational pressures frequently prevent managers from concentrating exclusively on such tasks, and some senior managements also find it difficult to focus on both operational and strategic problems at the same time. Management teams often get caught up in other matters or political battles, and progress can be delayed. Internal consultants provide a focused and dedicated resource to assist managers in overcoming these problems. Establishing project teams who focus exclusively on a project or task means that senior management time can be focused and used more effectively.

To secure a confidante

Some clients like to develop a consultant relationship in order that they can have access to a confidante. Being able to listen to a client's problems or issues in a range of disguises can be a much valued role for any internal consultant. In some instances you may be required simply to listen; to enable your client to express his or her views on an issue without passing judgement. In others you might be required to challenge or provoke your client's thinking; perhaps to consider alternative approaches or courses of action. This aspect of the internal consultant's role demands that you develop a relationship over a period of time. For clients who do not feel comfortable discussing sensitive issues with their peers or colleagues, it can be an extremely valued and powerful role for any internal consultant to perform.

To contribute to an important decision-making process

Where major decisions or projects are involved, managers may want to obtain additional input from consultants to help their decision-making processes. It may be that research or specialist technical information is required. This involves consultants drawing on their own experience or, alternatively, obtaining information from other sources, perhaps from outside the organization. It may be the case that your client is asking you to challenge or test a project or proposal to ensure that every possible issue has been addressed and thought through. Your involvement in such cases is likely to be limited to providing a very focused and technical input for a limited period of time.

To demonstrate that business opportunities are being identified and developed

Employing consultants on specific business projects is a method by which senior managers can demonstrate that their organization is maximizing all the opportunities available to it. Again, day-to-day operational pressures sometimes prevent managers from devoting the necessary time to explore and examine potential opportunities. Consultants offer the necessary flexibility of resource to enable managers to investigate new ventures.

Conversely, some managers who are under pressure or criticism from colleagues might employ consultants to demonstrate that they have a difficult situation under control. Clearly, this action might be interpreted as a negative use of consultants because it can involve them in complex and potentially hazardous organizational politics.

To reduce the risk of a project's failure

Where highly complex and expensive projects are concerned, the involvement of consultants with high-level expertise can obviously reduce the risk of a project running into difficulties. Employing specialist expertise or project management skills provided by consultants helps provide comfort to senior managers that an important project is being properly resourced, supported and managed. As well as providing the expertise, you may be acting as a comfort blanket to the organization.

Potentially negative uses of consultants

'Don't get killed too fast!'

Peter Brunner, Internal Consultant Company Development and Communications,
Mercedes-Benz AG

Of course, there are those instances where consultants can be used for negative or even subversive reasons or purposes. In such cases you need to be extremely cautious about getting involved, as the potential outcomes of these situations can have negative implications for your credibility and reputation. When this happens, your ability to operate successfully in your organization becomes seriously impaired.

To help undermine an existing management group or situation

In some situations a consultant might be employed to deliberately attack a specific proposal or initiative that has been sponsored by another manager or group. This can involve you in an acrimonious relationship and a 'no win' situation. There is a distinct difference between situations where you might be asked to critically evaluate or validate a proposal or action plan and those where there is a hidden political agenda that is not explained to you at the outset of a project. You should always probe to establish the reasons why your client has decided to involve you. If your suspicions are aroused, probe harder to uncover the real motives.

If you suspect or sense a difficult situation, you will need to explain your concerns to your prospective client. You need to point out the potential dilemmas you face in trying to operate successfully in the long term if you become involved in such a project. Always remember that if you are seen as someone who does the 'dirty work' of others, you will have problems when next trying to operate in other parts of your organization.

Providing management with support to justify previously agreed decisions or actions

'Avoid getting into the middle of power games.'

Peter Brunner, Internal Consultant Company Development and Communications,

Mercedes-Benz AG

In certain situations internal consultants may be asked to tackle assignments in order that a manager can justify an already agreed course of action by reference to a consultant's report or recommendation. This is not an unreasonable request, but as a matter of principle, and in your own self-interest, you should try to avoid such projects. Internal consultants must always safeguard their reputation and independence. Accepting work of this nature can influence people's views on your integrity. If you lose your integrity, your ability to operate successfully in the future will be seriously impaired. People who are suspicious of your motives and behaviours are unlikely to co-operate with you in providing information and assistance. As an internal consultant, you must try to avoid overtly political assignments.

To have someone to blame

While we have advocated the use of consultants on important projects, it is also the case that in some extreme situations certain managers will view the involvement of consultants as providing them with a convenient scapegoat in the event that a project does not produce a satisfactory outcome. In such situations it is critical that you secure your client's agreement to all stages of a project and that you manage their commitment throughout the project so as to avoid criticism at a later stage. If you sense that the situation is one where you will be unable to emerge without damage, you should avoid entering the project at the outset.

Managers might also use internal consultants to recommend or implement particularly difficult actions, such as staff reductions or business closures. The tactic can involve hiding behind the consultant's recommendations so as to push through the difficult process in the hope that the reputation of management will not be diminished. Suffice to say, people often see through the tactic, with the result that a management's reputation is often further damaged rather than enhanced.

However, there may be some legitimate reasons whereby a client might employ this tactic for some longer-term benefit which might not be immediately apparent. There are circumstances involving complex re-organizations and key staff deployments where it may be acceptable for a manager to refer to a consultant's recommendations. In such situations the manager may have in mind the stability of future working relationships and the need for the consultant to be fully recognized as the agent of the changes. Indeed, it can be argued that this method of using consultants is the act of a skilled and thoughtful manager trying to take a long-term and beneficial outlook on a difficult problem.

Clearly, none of these situations are easy to cope with or manage, so you need to weigh up carefully the potential benefits and losses involved and discuss these with your potential client before becoming involved in such projects.

HOW TO BECOME AN INTERNAL CONSULTANT

The manager

It is our belief that the skills contained in this book are highly relevant to any manager in a modern organization. The move from traditional command and control structures to more empowered working practices means that managers are increasingly becoming enablers or facilitators to their staff. The new role provides a means of support that allows people to develop and improve organizational performance without the need to feel dependent on conventional management powers. The consultancy model provides a viable means by which traditional managers can start to operate in this new mode. In that sense, any manager can start to use the approaches and skills detailed in this book. They have, as their underlying basis, the requirement to let people, or, in our jargon, clients, take responsibility and ownership for actions which you, as an internal consultant, may have assisted them in taking. So we would argue that these skills, and in particular the process skills of handling client relationships, can be employed not just on projects but also in day-to-day working relationships between managers and their staff. Clearly, it will be easier to utilize these skills if you are operating as a true internal consultant, but for the traditional manager there is much to adapt and apply in his or her existing working relationships.

The support function

Any support function can become an internal consultancy unit merely by possessing or having developed a body of knowledge, experience and skills in managing specialist activities or tackling difficult technical problems. However, in our experience there also needs to be an underlying organizational move towards developing an internal consulting capability. We outlined earlier how many support functions, such as information technology, are changing their operating methods to those of a consulting unit. These changes need to be accompanied by a clear communications strategy which sets out the rationale for introducing the role and the implications for managers and their working relationship with the new support function. It is not sufficient simply to change the role without communicating and educating managers about the new regime. Managers who have been used to a traditional form of support function will need to understand the new changes in service provision.

Some organizations which are aggressively pursuing the consulting concept have gone so far as to introduce new financial procedures which require line managers to contract with the consultancy unit for a project or assignment fee. Other organizations have changed the operating role without altering the funding or resourcing requirements. In either situation senior managers and those employed in the consultancy unit will need to ensure that they have communicated effectively with the rest of the organization. Failure to do so will invariably result in confusion and managers complaining about the new service provision. Any line manager who for fifteen years has picked up his or her telephone to the personnel or IT department and received an immediate response will react angrily the first time he or she is told that it will be a week before you can meet him or her. You have to inform managers clearly about the new role. It is a communication process that cannot be left to chance, and must involve a high-level dialogue with all managers throughout the organization.

> 'Remember that as an internal consultant you may be classified as an unknown quantity or a special animal; "an inside outsider" or "change agent". Also, you may be an object of curiosity or fear to other people in the organization.'
>
> *Dalim Basu*
> *Project Manager*
> *Independent Television Network*

TIME TO CONVERT AND REDIRECT

Embarking on this approach also demands time and patience. As we will explore in detail, operating as an internal consultant is very different from managing a traditional support function. In most organizations it is not possible simply to close down one day and start operating as a consultancy unit the next. Invariably, managers and functions require a period of adjustment.

> 'Development from a line manager to an internal consultant takes time so you need to have a belief in what you are doing. You need to adjust your style to suit the situation and be prepared to be alone.'
>
> *Peter Stewart*
> *Business Development Manager*
> *PowerGen UK*

You will need time to convert from the old to the new and recognize that there will be tensions in making the transition. These changes require careful planning, as you and your former customers will need to adjust to a new working relationship.

In addition to possessing functional or specialist expertise, consulting skills also require the ability to collect and analyse information, develop options and recommend practical and workable solutions and action plans. You also need to keep pace with the latest developments, methodologies and techniques in your specialist field of expertise. The continuous development of your skills and knowledge base is a critical means by which you achieve credibility and influence with clients. It is only over a gradual period of time that you can expect to make the transition, and you will need to be realistic about the time this will take.

'You must be balanced. You should be a good learner, who can turn information into knowledge. You should be a good listener, willing to suspend judgement in order to make a good judgement. You should be able to motivate yourself. An internal consultant must like working with people; when a client irritates you, focus on the behaviour and not on the person.

Most of all, it is very important to look after your own personal and professional development: read the trade journals, attend training programmes, monitor your own physical and mental energy, be aware of your own stress threshold, from time to time give yourself a week to recharge.

I would recommend attending two programmes on professional development and at least one on personal development each year. Your cutting edge will become blunter and blunter, and your work less effective unless you take time to sharpen the saw.'

Anisa Caine
Personal Development
Consultant
Peak Potential

2 Key stages of the internal consulting process

THE KEY STAGES OF THE INTERNAL CONSULTING PROCESS

In this chapter we outline the key stages and activities involved in managing successful projects. Our consulting process involves a systematic approach to managing projects or assignments which ensures that you not only deliver successful results but that you also enjoy strong and positive client relationships. The skills involved in managing projects can also be applied in lots of day-to-day working relationships between managers and their staff. Making a successful transition from colleague to client requires the careful application of these consulting stages.

A consultancy project or assignment can be divided into five key stages, with a sixth stage that continues throughout the duration of a project. These stages are shown in Figure 2.1 and involve:

1. Getting in and contracting with your client
2. Understanding and defining your client's problem
3. Action planning
4. Implementation
5. Reviewing and exiting the project
6. Presenting client feedback.

As an internal consultant, it is likely that in most cases you will be expected to get involved in all these stages. However, it is important to remember that on some assignments your participation in stages 3 (action planning) and 4 (implementation) may be reduced, as your client may decide to take on these responsibilities. For example, if you were asked to carry out a departmental structure review you would almost certainly carry out stages 1 (getting in with your client), 2 (understanding the problem), 6 (presenting client feedback) and then carry out stage 5 (reviewing and exiting), whereas the

> 'Our success is based on client satisfaction. Our activities must be client focused. Our teams are visitors to our operating companies, providing the best possible service, listening to people and not sounding like experts. However, we aim to drive for implementation with speed and urgency.'
>
> *Curt Blattner*
> *Head, Productivity Team*
> *Nestlé Group, Switzerland*

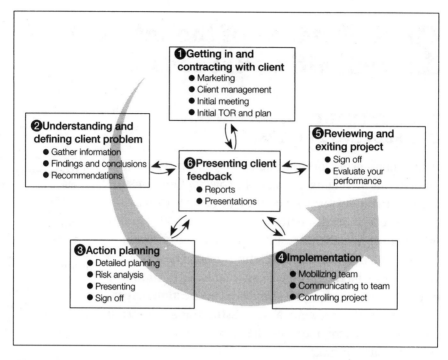

Figure 2.1 *The internal consulting process*

client and their key staff might take over stage 3 (action planning) and manage stage 4 (implementation) involving the new department structure.

A crucial point to remember is that no two projects or assignments are ever the same and that, as an internal consultant, you must remain flexible and responsive to your client's needs and demands. Some clients will want to rely heavily on your services throughout the duration of a project. Conversely, others may want to reduce their dependency on you by absorbing much of the work involved in any action planning and implementation phases. As an internal consultant, you need to be comfortable with both arrangements. You should not feel personally rejected if your client decides to reduce your involvement in this latter stage of a project, unless, of course, you have done something negative to justify your exclusion.

Getting in and contracting with your client

As an internal consultant, you have to have a group of potential clients who recognize your expertise and are willing to involve you in projects or initiatives when suitable opportunities arise. Your ability to generate interest in your skills and services is the first step in obtaining invitations to discuss the provision of help or assistance with potential clients. To succeed in this challenge, you will have to market yourself and, where appropriate, your team or unit's services.

Marketing internal consultancy

For the new or inexperienced consultant, the prospect of having to go out into the organization and actively market or sell his or her services can come as a shock, but the fact is, internal consultancy demands this approach. If your organization is unaware of who you are and what you can offer, the chances of you being asked to discuss problems and provide advice to clients will be remote. If you cannot rely on potential clients coming to you, then marketing your services becomes an essential and on-going task. This marketing stance represents a significant departure from the work of many traditional managers and support functions who have enjoyed a captive market for their services.

In our chapter on marketing we outline some of the specific actions you can take to begin the marketing process in your organization. These include developing a simple marketing strategy and promoting your skills and services to senior management.

When your marketing efforts have been successful, a potential client will invite you to a meeting to discuss a particular issue or problem and to explore whether you might be able to provide some assistance. This is your selling opportunity, and for most internal consultants the probability is that you will have worked for this person before, either in providing some form of management or functional support. However, to succeed as an internal consultant you will need to manage this person in a different manner than in the past.

Initial client meetings

Initial client meetings represent the start of our client management process and the move from colleague to client relationship. There are several important guidelines you need to follow to produce a successful result and secure your client's agreement to the next stage of a project.

The purpose of any initial client meeting is for you to begin to understand your client's business. This involves jointly exploring problem areas and establishing the possible basis for a project or assignment, together with provisional objectives and timescales. At this stage of your relationship, you might also discuss the possible involvement of your client's staff in the work and any requirements for specialist skills such as finance, human resources, project management, production, engineering, logistics, information technology, etc.

When starting out as a new internal consultant, you may have to begin redefining past relationships with some of your clients so that they see your involvement on an equal partnership basis. Your clients may have viewed your previous role as that of a subservient support function, and if you are going to command the respect and authority you need to become a successful consultant, you will have to shift any negative perceptions. As an internal consultant, you want to have a strong and mutually respectful relationship with all your clients. But, depending on your starting point, this may take time, and you will need to be patient in order to build up a range of positive successes to change people's attitudes. This process of influencing your clients' perceptions and attitudes begins at the initial meeting stage.

Developing initial terms of reference

On the basis that both you and your client have had a satisfactory meeting and agreed in principle to start working together, you must then produce initial terms of reference that can be discussed and agreed at your next meeting. In many situations you may need to carry out some preliminary research to define the precise scope of the problem, although for some simple and straightforward assignments it may be possible to agree the initial terms of reference at your initial client meeting.

Agreeing initial terms of reference with your client before you begin any consulting work is a fundamental rule in managing all your client relationships. You and your client must be absolutely clear about the boundary and objectives of a project at the outset. The process of agreeing initial terms of reference ensures that a clear and mutual understanding has taken place. Many consultants have met with failure and ultimately faced an angry client because they ignored this rule and assumed that a lack of clarity or understanding at this initial stage would not matter in the later stages of a project. The fact is that it matters a great deal. Clients and consultants can misunderstand or forget the details of initial discussions. This can be further exacerbated if any agreements are not documented. Establishing an initial terms of reference is the means by which you establish a clear focus on what your client wants and agrees to. It is also a process that helps develop your client's thinking about their problem and what it is exactly that they want from you. Very often, a client's view of a problem can change significantly as a result of a consultant probing and challenging them at an initial meeting. So the process is intended to benefit both parties by ensuring that there is a clear under-standing of the aims of a project. This helps prevent any surprises at a later stage.

As your work develops on a project, you will con-stantly need to refer to your terms of reference. When circumstances surrounding a project change, you may well need to adjust the overall objectives. This is why we refer to 'initial' terms of reference at the beginning of a project, as it is very likely that they will change, especially where you become involved in complex imple-mentation work which will require detailed planning schedules.

In developing your initial terms of reference you should include the following information:

- Background to the project
- Objectives of the project
- Boundary of the project
- Constraints involved
- Assumptions you are making at this stage
- Client's reporting requirements
- Project deliverables and milestones
- Show who and when things happen on an activity time chart
- Finance required to carry out the project.

In most cases, to understand fully your client's problem you will need to complete a brief but intensive period of fact finding. This may involve you interviewing a small cross-section of people or conducting some form of research. You have to make sure that you under-stand the background to your client's problems so that you can provide an initial estimate of the resources and time you will need to complete the project. When your terms of reference are agreed with your client, they in effect become your consulting contract. They also become the basis on which your eventual success or failure will be judged, which is why they assume such significance in the client management process. Without clearly agreed terms of reference you cannot hope to deliver effective consulting services.

INSIGHT

Never lose focus of your terms of reference, and keep them readily available throughout the course of any project. On complex or lengthy assignments it is very easy to lose sight of your original objectives and stray from your terms of reference. This can be very damaging, either towards the end of an assignment or when you have to report back at key stages. You do not want your client to feel that you have not delivered, so keep asking yourself and your colleagues, 'Have we done what we said we would do?'

On some projects you will be required to bid for the work and compete with other groups, possibly external consultants. Preparing initial terms of reference will not be enough, as you will have to prepare a client proposal. This is a more formal document which will include your initial terms of reference as well as the following sections:

- Consulting experience – document your experience and skills and that of the team
- Methodology – describe your approach to executing the work.

INSIGHT

Consultants always leave insufficient time for drafting and producing client reports. A useful guide in planning is simply to double the time you think you will need! You can never do enough drafting and editing of a final report.

Understanding and defining your client's problem

In the majority of assignments or projects a detailed period of fact finding will be necessary to ensure that you are obtaining the correct information in order to understand and accurately define your client's problem. This requires you to be inquisitive and open-minded throughout your investigative approach. Simply accepting what is said to you without challenging or questioning the issues may result in you developing erroneous findings and conclusions. You also need to develop a structured and analytical approach to ensure that all the relevant facts and issues are established and understood. Having a clear understanding of the information gathered during the initial stages of your work will also help you to highlight additional areas which may require further investigation. Ultimately, you must be able to develop valid conclusions and recommendations from all your facts.

The main methods of gathering information are:

- desk research, which typically involves the review

and examination of existing information or records (e.g. current reports, efficiency statistics, systems outputs, policies, operating procedures and sales or customer data, etc.)

- interviews conducted on an individual basis
- group interviews
- questionnaires circulated to staff, customers, suppliers or other relevant parties
- process mapping.

Most consultancy projects will involve a combination of all these methods. Interviews are, of course, always critical in gathering information and it is impossible to carry out consulting work without having to interview some people. When conducting client interviews you must always:

- be professional, respectful and courteous
- have a checklist of the main questions and issues you want to discuss
- remain impartial (never criticizing client staff or others within the organization and never being drawn into making controversial statements)
- distinguish clearly between information that is given to you 'on the record' and 'off the record'.

To be successful, interviews need to be conducted in a relaxed and open atmosphere. There may also be moments when you need to maintain client confidentiality with regard to personal 'off the record' comments. You may need to protect people who share confidential information with you by giving assurances that you are only identifying broad themes and issues rather than attributing specific comments to individuals.

Action planning

Action planning is the stage of the consulting process which requires you to develop detailed plans for achieving your project's objectives. On some projects your involvement may well end at this stage, with your client taking over control. If your involvement in a project does end at this stage, you must be aware that, as far as your client is concerned, the project is not finished. Completion of your review or the delivery of a report frequently represents a beginning, not an end, for your client.

On very large and complex projects involving, for example, a major information systems implementation, your client will frequently have to manage a large workload, and it may be necessary to involve a specialist project manager to carry out the detailed planning and monitoring activities. In such situations large numbers of people and resources will be involved, and this demands a more disciplined and rigorous approach to project management. However, in the majority of consulting projects the responsibility for carrying out the detailed planning and implementation management will lie with you as the internal consultant in charge of the project. So you have to be prepared to take on the role and develop some of the skills of a project manager.

INSIGHT

Identify and involve all the appropriate people who will participate in the planning discussions. These are the people who will ultimately assume responsibility for any new systems or procedures, so their active involvement must be secured. As a minimum, these people will include your client, their management team and any other key people who will implement the system or changes.

Action planning involves the following steps:

- Assessing your project management skills
- Assessing how much planning you need to do
- Reaffirming your terms of reference
- Preparing a quick activity time chart
- Carrying out a risk analysis
- Preparing a detailed activity time chart for a high-risk project
- Presenting your plan to your client
- Getting your client to sign off.

Not all these steps need to be carried out, and identifying the ones you need to apply yourself to is discussed in detail in our chapter on action planning.

Implementation

At this stage the main work is carried out to meet the objectives of the project, and you need to make things happen using your terms of reference and activity time chart. The implementation process is made up of the following three steps:

- Mobilizing the team
- Communicating to the team
- Controlling the project.

Mobilizing the team

At this stage your project team and all the other necessary resources you require for your action plan are contacted and mobilized. You confirm with key people that they will be working on the project and begin the process of motivating them towards the objectives. In some cases you will be asked to take on the overall management of the implementation process, perhaps being supported by an expert project manager. In other assignments you may be asked to provide assistance on a less involved basis. In either situation your involvement during the implementation stage is important because very often only you and your client will have an overall understanding of the project's background and aims.

Communicating to the team

During any implementation phase it is important that you prepare a thorough communications pack and distribute this to the implementation team so that they are all informed of the project objectives and time-scales. You should also prepare and distribute a mini terms of reference and a summary activity time chart. Everyone involved in the implementation process needs to be clearly aware of your client's requirements. You will need to allocate detailed tasks to each team member so that they know what they have to do in addition to possessing a full understanding of the project's overall goals.

Controlling the project

Once your project gets under way, your main responsibility is to ensure that the plan is implemented so that the objectives in your terms of reference are met. You therefore have constantly to focus on your project's objectives by:

- tracking the team's progress against the plan
- reviewing the plan
- replanning to meet the project objectives.

The process of tracking the team's progress against the plan enables you to find out what tasks have been completed and what work remains. This will take up a considerable amount of your time, but the information gathered will help to keep your project on course. Record your team's progress on your activity time chart, which will be used when reviewing and replanning parts of the project.

Successful project reviews are best achieved by holding regular review meetings, and result in any decisions being fully documented and agreed action points circulated to everyone involved in the project. Structured progress meetings also ensure that your client is kept fully informed of the work being undertaken and of the project's overall progress and development. It also means that you can highlight any problem areas at an early stage. It is vital that you keep your client involved at all times, so as to manage their commitment throughout the implementation phase.

Finally, replanning may take place after holding your review meetings. You need to record any new or changed tasks on your activity time chart and also change your terms of reference if appropriate. In some cases you may decide that no changes to your plan are needed. Alternatively, you may have to consider a number of alternative options, such as offering incentives or increasing resources, before replanning parts of your project plan in order to keep it on track.

During the implementation phase of a project you should never rely solely on written forms of communication. Utilize face-to-face communications as much as possible to ensure that people have fully understood the issues and their objectives. Any internal consultant who believes that by simply writing a memorandum he or she has communicated is making a big assumption and more probably a bigger mistake at some future stage. You must keep people informed by carrying out effective and timely briefings and allowing people to raise issues and problem areas. Reporting documents should not become a substitute for direct face-to-face reporting. On projects that are running into difficulties, written communications can sometimes become a form of self-defence, so be wary of relying solely on the written word.

Reviewing and exiting projects

As a successful internal consultant, your time will be at a premium, with many clients requesting your services, so you have to manage their expectations with regard to your availability. If you allow your clients to believe that they have endless freedom to demand your services at any time, you will never be able to operate successfully as you will end up with conflicting client commitments. So, at the end of an assignment, you must inform your client that your involvement has come to an end and that any additional work will have to be subject to a new agreement. You also need to assess whether or not the project has been successful and delivered the results according to your original terms of reference. The most appropriate way to do this is to present your client with a report that will include:

- a review of various aspects of the project
- a review of your performance.

This review process can also involve identifying additional or further actions that might be required to achieve a project's final objectives. It might, in some circumstances, identify who should undertake any additional work and specify the timescales involved. The review process should always be undertaken in partnership with your client. This approach is a positive sign which shows that the project was conducted in a mature and professional manner where both the client and the consultant accepted their responsibilities for the outcome. Our toolkit chapter presents a number of forms to help you work through and manage this process.

Presenting client feedback

'Communicate bad news early – never cover up.'

Tony Edgar, Senior Manager, Lloyds Bank

Presenting client feedback is a phase of the consulting process that runs throughout the life cycle of any project or assignment with which you are involved. Client feedback must take place regularly during any project to ensure that your client is kept up-to-date on progress and advised of any difficulties at a sooner rather than a later stage. Any consultant who neglects this part of the consulting cycle is likely to run into problems sooner or later.

You must always take the initiative when communicating with your client. Never be in the position where your client is chasing you for information or progress updates. If you find yourself in such a situation it probably means that you have failed to pay sufficient attention to the feedback process of your client relationship. When it comes to feedback and progress reports always stay one step ahead of your client. Never, ever try to hide problems or delay giving bad news, as it always makes the situation worse.

Any project completion date ultimately results in some form of final report or client presentation. During this stage of the feedback process your client is looking to assess the quality and integrity of your work, and you in turn are looking to gauge their reactions. It is also the stage at which you will be aiming to further strengthen your client relationship by securing agreement to your findings, conclusions and recommendations.

The two major activities involved in presenting client feedback will involve you in writing reports and making formal presentations. They constitute two critical skill areas that must be mastered, as poor performances in either can seriously erode or damage your overall performance and your client's confidence in your overall ability and competence.

Writing client reports

Any client report must be a clear statement of what you set out to do, what you did, your recommendations and, where appropriate, your proposed implementation plans. As an internal consultant, your report must be capable of being understood at a first reading by anyone who does not possess a detailed knowledge of the problem or issues under review.

Report writing is a complex and at times painful process, but there is no escaping from the discipline that must be applied. All consultants experience difficulty at one time or another in writing reports, so you should not be too depressed when you find yourself struggling with a complex report. But you must recognize that there is a significant difference in the skills needed to analyse a complex problem and then to write a clear and logical report on the situation. However, both sets of skills are necessary to produce a report which is rigorous in analysis and clear in presentation. In many projects your final report is often the only way in which your client can or will judge your performance, so you have to display a high degree of skill and capability.

Making client presentations

While your conclusions and recommendations should always be discussed with your client in advance of your final report being submitted, there invariably comes a time when you will be expected to make a formal presentation on your work to your client.

When working on sensitive projects you should always personally present your report rather than send it to your client. This allows you to clarify any potentially contentious or difficult issues immediately. Client presentations are one of the most important parts of an internal consultant's work, and during the latter stages of a project they become critical, as they provide you with the opportunity to explain issues in your report that might not be immediately clear to your client and so lie open to misinterpretation. Following any client presentation that you give, you may need to consider reviewing and possibly amending your final report in the light of the comments received during your presentation.

Like report writing, client presentations can be extremely complex events and you can never plan or prepare enough for them. During any presentation you may have to deal with sensitive issues involving criticism of your client or other managers or departments. You may also have to safeguard confidential issues which emerged during your work. When issues such as these are present, you will not only have to plan for them but also think about how you will manage them during your actual presentation. As such, you will need to be skilled not only in structuring presentations but also in planning around detailed process issues. For example, how do you deal with the fact that attending your presentation might be two managers who you know to be extremely hostile to what you have to report? Dealing with this type of issue is an everyday challenge for the internal consultant. In our client presentation section we will outline some of the techniques you can use to ensure that you manage such situations and secure your client's support and commitment at the feedback stage.

3 Getting in and contracting with your client

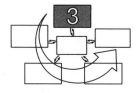

MARKETING INTERNAL CONSULTANCY

The first stage in our consulting cycle involves getting in front of some potential clients in order to discuss the possibility of providing some kind of assistance. In moving from a conventional managerial role or support function to an internal consultancy approach you will therefore need to plan how you are going to sell your services to the rest of your organization. In effect, you will need to market yourself. For people new to the consultancy role, this can be a major departure from past practices. Having actively to promote your services as opposed to having a readily available stream of internal customers can come as a major challenge. Of course whether or not you need to promote your services aggressively will depend on the operating guidelines your organization has given you. In many instances you may simply have to market your services on a small scale, having still been guaranteed a regular amount of work. Conversely, you may find yourself in a very competitive situation and having to compete with external consultants. In this case you will have almost to continually promote your services in order to ensure a steady supply of internal client enquiries and requests.

The first step in developing your marketing strategy involves answering some questions concerning your role and contribution. This demands that you step back from any day-to-day commitments and look fundamentally at your future objectives and aims. If you are going to be working in a consulting team you will need to discuss these issues with your colleagues. To complete this task, you might consider spending a couple of hours together or even a full day so that you can develop your responses to the following questions:

> 'Be where your clients are – make regular visits no matter how far away they are, even if you do not have a pretence. Important issues often come up in casual conversation.'
>
> *Marcia Hershkovitz*
> *Human Resource Specialist*
> *Novo Nordisk*

- What type of consulting business are we in?
- Who are our clients?
- What are their needs?
- What are the results and benefits of our services?
- What are our qualities?
- What are our objectives as a consulting unit?
- What potential barriers or obstacles exist for us?
- Who are our competitors?
- What risks are involved?
- What overall strategy should we adopt to become successful?

You might also conduct a client demand area analysis which identifies who your various clients are and what it is they actually want from you in terms of services. Figure 3.1 shows an example form.

In completing this analysis you are required to think

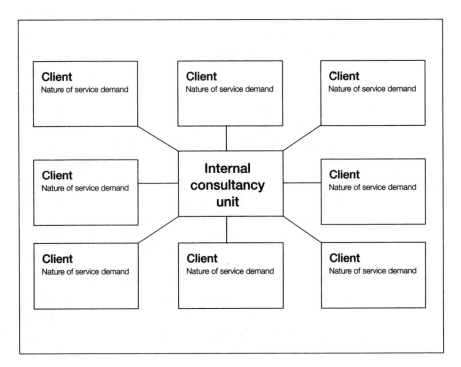

Figure 3.1 *Demand area analysis – assessing your client's needs*

of every possible client group that you serve and to determine what it is that you provide them with, be it a service, information, advice or some other form of assistance. This form of analysis can be very powerful, as it forces you to consider your various clients and the extent to which you currently satisfy their needs. As a result of your analysis, you may find yourself focusing on some clients more than others. You may even find yourself deciding to reduce your services to certain clients if you conclude that they will not serve your success in the long term. So be prepared to have to make some tough decisions in order to get the right focus.

Not only addressing but answering these questions demands a high degree of self-analysis and criticism. It is no use thinking that everything you do is worthwhile and excellent if your clients have a different perspective. In order to generate real focus on what you need to do to become successful, you must question all your activities. You have to be clear as to your starting base and evaluate your previous track record.

You can then begin to determine how you are going to operate and function as an internal consultancy group by tackling some of the questions listed below. They are designed to get you to think about the day-to-day aspects of operating as a consultant and to develop a consistent approach. As with all strategic planning type processes, there are no right or wrong answers and you can obtain maximum benefit by working through these questions with your colleagues. The questions will help you to structure your thoughts and discussions and, in so doing, you will be forced to review your situation and assess the facts surrounding your group. Ultimately, you will need to make clear decisions about your operating role, but you should emerge with a clear focus and sense of direction.

For illustrative purposes we have included a cross-section of example answers to the key questions. These cover possible responses from groups as diverse as training through to information technology departments. Ultimately, however, there are no simple answers. You and your colleagues have to do all the thinking, as only you can come up with the relevant responses to develop a strategy that is appropriate for your specific operation.

Developing your marketing strategy

What sort of consulting group are we?

We are a small highly focused consulting team providing value added services in the areas of systems design and support. We specialize in the development of UNIX-based applications to enhance organizational efficiency and business performance.

Who are our clients?

Our clients are the senior executive and middle management groups across the organization.

What do our clients require from us?

Our clients require a highly flexible and responsive service in the area of information technology. They equally demand a level of technical support that compares with the best that is available externally.

What services and products do we provide?

We provide a range of training and people development solutions as well as a portfolio of skills development programmes, self-development and learning resources – which also includes distance learning packages, videos, books and audio tapes.

What is our clients' perception of us?

Our client image is that of a high-quality and customer-responsive unit that delivers real value added solutions on limited resources.

How do our clients regard our value to them?

Our client perception of 'our prices' and value is that we are relatively inexpensive in comparison with external service providers.

How do we intend to develop our client base?

We will seek more work through our existing client base. We do not propose to develop new streams of client activity at this particular stage of our development.

How will we operate and distribute our services?

We plan to provide and deliver our services by allocating a dedicated individual to each business unit. This will ensure that every manager has a direct contact to our services and is met by someone who shares a close understanding of his or her business and operating environment.

How will we communicate and promote our services?

We will promote our services through our existing client base and by actively promoting our successes through the organization's various seminars, newsletters and promotional literature. We also propose to run a series of workshops on a regular basis to update our clients on our latest service offerings.

Financial/budgetary objectives

We will achieve the following objectives in line with our agreed operating guidelines which are to recover our total operating costs from our internal, and wherever possible, external consulting activities.

'Understand your organization's decision making processes and who the key decision maker is. Remember the ultimate responsibility may not rest with the immediate sponsor so it is important to know the authority levels of various sponsors.'

Lewis Doyle
Business Development Manager
Legal and General

What clients look for

To develop even more detailed responses to the above questions, you will need to put yourself in your client's shoes and ask yourself, 'Why should I buy from these people?' This is an immensely powerful question to ask yourself as a consultant. You must think about your client's needs and focus on what your client is looking for when selecting consultants to work with them.

Tangibles

Clients look for tangibles such as performance and efficiency improvements, reduced costs, improved revenues, enhanced levels of customer service, etc. These are the factors that will get your clients interested, so try to harness your marketing efforts to focus on them.

Business understanding

Clients buy from people who they feel understand their problems and issues. So question whether you do display a clear and comprehensive understanding of your client's business. If not, start developing your knowledge base and try to find out as much as you can about the challenges facing your client.

Methodologies

Many clients are impressed by proven methodologies which detail precise ways of working and implementing change. They provide clients with a degree of comfort that the consultant is professional and knows what he or she is doing. Methodologies are quite common in the area of information technology, but can be and are adopted in other areas, such as training and development and, of course, production methods. So be alert to the possibilities of using or adapting such techniques to your field of work.

Reassurance

Clients who buy consultancy services are putting themselves at risk, as they are placing their confidence and trust in someone who they may not know too well. Your client may therefore need reassurance of your competence and your success in applying solutions to their problem. After hiring you, many clients will be asking themselves whether they have done the right thing. Clients like to have confidence and peace of mind with regard to their decisions. So deal with these less tangible aspects of client satisfaction by keeping close to your client, advising them of progress and

Example of consulting team operating statement

- 'Use the Nestec Productivity Team (NPT) as a career development step
- Commitment, Credibility, Confidence = 3Cs:
- Find synergies (most wheels have been invented)
- Use the brainpower of our employees
- "We know how but don't apply"
- Focus on the how not the what – "it's not just what you do, it's the way you do it"
- Stop! Before compromising commitment.'

Operating Statement Nestlé Group Productivity Team Vevey, Switzerland

Courtesy of Curt Blattner

offering constant reassurance. Staying close to your clients and being proactive in keeping them up-to-date is central to promoting the 'right' feelings.

But if that is what clients look for, *what is it* that they are actually buying? Well, there are two critical things that clients are buying from you as an internal consultant.

The resolution of needs

Part of your role as a consultant will be to help your client translate their broad concerns and issues into specific needs which can then be satisfied through your intervention and combined actions. A large part of successful consultancy involves focusing your client's thoughts so as to uncover their real needs – as that is ultimately what they want addressed. So often, a client is not clear as to what it is they want. That is why you must devote a lot of time in the initial stages of your client relationship probing and identifying the real problem areas. What clients initially say they want may not ultimately be what they need. Your initial involvement with a client often involves trying to resolve and define their real underlying needs.

Solutions

Ultimately, clients want solutions to their problems. Products or methodologies that assist you in this process are valuable, but you should never lose sight of the fact that it is the solution that matters most to your client. Therefore, when shaping your marketing approaches, focus on how your involvement can help your client to address and solve their problems.

INSIGHT

Never, ever confuse what you are trying to sell as a consultant with what your client wants to buy. You must always address your client's real needs and not what you think they need. Following this golden rule will ensure that you stay client focused.

Beginning to market yourself: recognizing your starting point

Figure 3.2 illustrates the range of potential client reactions that might greet any marketing activity you conduct. Clearly, it makes sense to focus efforts on those clients who either express a genuine interest in your services or actively seek your assistance. In the longer term you will also need to remain in touch with those potential clients who are aware of your services but who have not requested any help. You cannot afford to ignore these clients as they may represent a valuable source of future work for you. Indeed, you may well need to spend time trying to understand why they have not contacted you. But be wary of expending lots of energy and effort on people who have no intention of ever wanting to use your services.

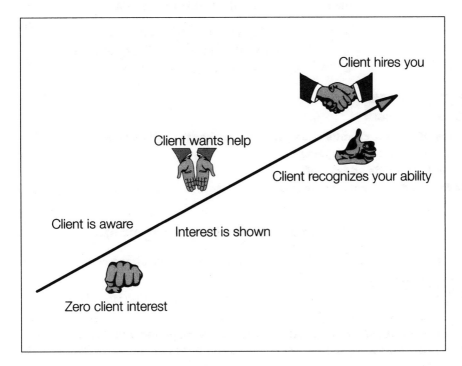

Figure 3.2   *Recognize your starting point*

Marketing to senior management

'Aim high in your organization – if you want to get things done you need the support and involvement of top management.'

Marcia Hershkovitz, Human Resources Specialist, Novo Nordisk

Who are your key clients?

When trying to focus your marketing activities, reflect on the classic Pareto Principle of 80–20. In marketing terms this suggests that 20 per cent of your clients account for 80 per cent of your workload and success. The question you need to address is whether you know which 20 per cent of your client base is delivering that output. So try to be always questioning and analysing your marketing approach to test its effectiveness. In most organizations an important element of that 20 per cent is likely to be senior management. By concentrating your marketing efforts on senior management you can gain the following benefits:

- Fewer but higher value added projects
- Referrals to other parts of the organization
- Access to strong sources of influence.

INSIGHT

Put yourself in your client's shoes and remember that all clients want to:
- **Feel important and respected**
- **Have their needs addressed**
- **Understand how you can help them.**

How to sell to senior management

'Get involved in the highest levels of operational meetings your clients conduct.'

Enid Murphy, Internal Consultant, Telstra Australia

'If you cannot add value say so, don't go through the motions and jeopardise your reputation.'

Mike Gelder, Divisional Manager, Lloyds Bank

When selling to senior management, there are three key steps to follow.

Understand your client's motives

You will need to identify at an early stage who the key decision makers will be in the selection process. Once you have identified them (often there will be more than one key manager involved), you should try to identify their individual needs and wants. Remember, not everyone is motivated by the same thing, so you need to examine whether their needs involve solving the problem, exploiting opportunities or securing personal credit. Do not overlook the desire for personal gain, as many senior managers may be looking for projects that can make them look good in their organization. By focusing on these different types of needs you can greatly enhance your success in selling your involvement.

Define the business priorities

By skilfully defining your client's key business priorities you can more easily identify the outputs or deliverables that your client is seeking to achieve as a result of your input. You should always try to reflect these priorities in your terms of reference so that your client can instantly recognize them. This will further impress your client and lead them to commit to your approach and involvement.

State the benefits of your involvement

Stating the benefits of your involvement to a client is where you have actively to argue your case. A powerful focus on the results or outputs of your work is what is required. Focusing only on the features of your involvement is a classic mistake. Marketing people always distinguish between features and benefits. Features are merely aspects of your approach, such as 'we use the latest technology!' or 'we have a detailed methodology' – these are all very interesting, but what your client really wants to hear is what that technology will do to help solve their problem. A benefit of using the latest technology may be that it will produce a faster and quicker solution. That is of more interest to your client. So always stay results-focused.

> 'Your client's time is precious, so it is essential that you do not waste their time by paraphrasing or reiterating what they already know. You must add value.'
>
> *Mike Gelder*
> *Divisional Manager*
> *Lloyds Bank*

Some practical tips to improve your marketing effort

> 'Always connect your services to your client's business objectives. Don't conduct management workshops without a real need. Action learning is the most successful approach to adopt.'
>
> *Peter Brunner*
> *Internal Consultant*
> *Company Development and*
> *Communications*
> *Mercedes-Benz AG*

- Solve the problems of your Chief Executive

- Focus on your organization's pressure points – find out where the business is hurting and see if you can help. It always pays to be business- and performance-focused

- Use factual bottom-line business performance measures to promote your activities – demonstrate a real value added contribution

- Work with those managers who are converted to your approach and services. Don't waste valuable time and effort on managers who will never understand or appreciate your work. Focus on people who value your input

- Cultivate word of mouth referrals. The best form of marketing (as well as the cheapest) is recommendations from happy and satisfied clients. So cultivate your clients to promote your work around the organization

- Think about developing a distinct identity in your organization. Discuss the possibility of promoting a logo or newsletter which informs the organization about your role and services

- Seize opportunities to present your good work. If asked to make a presentation at the annual conference, don't refuse. See it as an opportunity to talk about a successful project. If possible, do the presentation in partnership with the client

- Audit your staff to check that they are displaying client-focused skills. All your efforts can be wasted if the person answering your phone is less than professional towards existing and potential clients

- Develop your own personal network of contacts both internally and external to your organization. Take people out to lunch and talk about your projects

- Invite external speakers into your organization and invite influential managers along. It helps to position yourself as someone who is trying to add value to the organization

- Visit other companies and organizations. Find out about best practice in your field of operation. Your ability to comment on such matters gives you influence

- Collaborate with other internal consultants from other organizations. They can help improve your skill base and give you new ideas

- Send articles relevant to your work or of general business interest to key clients. It is a way of keeping yourself in front of them, and if the article is relevant they may well mention it next time you meet; alternatively, you have something that you can raise casually. Even better, however, you may find that your client actually asks you to follow up on some of the points contained in the article

- Keep a clear record of all your client meetings and don't lose touch with them. Clients do not like consultants who ring up because they have run out of work as it gives them a negative perception of how you value them and view them. Effective consultants work hard at maintaining relationships even when no work is on offer. You must always be thinking about the longer term and remember all client contact is a form of marketing

- Remember that most business comes from your existing client base. So try actively to promote your work and keep your clients in touch with other types of work you are engaged in

- Finally, stay alert to all opportunities. Any project, no matter how small, has the potential to develop into other areas and larger assignments.

'Talk the right language
Senior management –
justify with reasons,
earning before interest
and tax
Middle management –
cost savings, reductions
in operating costs and
efficiency
Operative staff – time
savings and making the
job easier.'

Robin Lanman
National Training and Quality
Manager
Mayne Nickless Courier Systems

INITIAL CLIENT MEETINGS

'Listen and have an element of curiosity.
Don't jump to conclusions or make assumptions.'
Influence but don't manipulate'

David Ohlmüs, Human Resource Consultant, Department of Immigration and Ethnic
Affairs, Australia

Initial client meetings are the starting point from which you begin building a client base in your organization. In most cases you will have been invited by a potential or existing client to discuss a problem and explore the possibility of providing some assistance. Your ability to handle and manage initial client meetings professionally is vital to your success.

Initial meetings are the first step in promoting your involvement and expertise to clients. Having the capability to enter a potential client's office and subsequently emerge having begun developing a business relationship or having sold your services is a demanding and challenging role. As an internal consultant, it may well be the case that you know your potential client. However, you need to be wary of making assumptions about how you deal with your clients. It is very easy for you to think that someone you have worked with for many years is simply an old colleague and that you do not need to change the way in which you conduct a meeting with him or her. This is not the approach to take. You need to view former colleagues with a very different 'client' perspective.

Initial meetings must be conducted professionally. Throughout the meeting you must send strong messages to your potential client that you value and appreciate their time. You have to show them that you are keen to assist them with any problems or challenges they may be facing. Simply arriving at someone's office with the intention of having a friendly discussion is not the way you impress clients that you are the right person to help them. Initial meetings are the first major step in developing and building a client relationship, so you have to make sure that you present the right image.

The objectives of initial client meetings are to:

- learn about your client's operation
- understand your clients problems or challenges
- determine whether you might be able to help them
- assess whether you can provide assistance in the necessary timescales
- assess whether you are interested in the problem
- begin building a client relationship
- reflect on your client's problem
- agree the next steps or withdraw from any further involvement.

The essential rules for managing initial client meetings

'Listen, listen, listen. This is the most important advice of all.'
Marcia Hershkovitz, Human Resources Specialist, Novo Nordisk

The most important rule in any initial meeting is to get your client talking. Getting through an initial meeting in a thorough and professional manner requires you to follow a set of clear guidelines. If you adhere to them, you will find that your initial meetings run smoothly and successfully:

- Always arrive on time – never be late, even if your client is (remember, that is their privilege)
- Introduce your colleagues (if two consultants are interviewing)
  - Carry out clear and focused introductions – who you are, where you are from, the nature of your skills
- Outline your understanding of the broad purpose and objectives of the meeting
- Check the time your client has available for the meeting

INSIGHT

A powerful question to ask your client at all initial meetings is, 'What would success look like if this project were to be successful and work?' It can be followed by, 'And what would people be doing differently as a result of the proposed initiative – what would they be doing that they are not doing now?'

● **In most instances these questions will secure powerful responses from your client. They will define in their own terms exactly what they want the project or your involvement to deliver. You will be surprised how quickly you obtain your client's fundamental requirements.**

● Obtain your client's agreement to the meeting's objectives and timescales – this forms the basis of a contract for your meeting. You want to find out as much as you can about your client's situation

● Discuss and clarify your understanding of the issues by asking lots of open-ended questions

● Summarize and reflect back your client's comments regularly to ensure that you have understood what has been said

● Ask for access to any supporting or relevant materials concerning the problem (reports, documents, etc. that might be supplied during or after your meeting)

● Check for any areas that your client does not want you to get involved in. Establish the boundaries to your work

● Agree on the results your client would like to achieve

● Be prepared to explore tentative ways to possibly solve your client's problem, remembering that it is very early to start being prescriptive about solutions

● Summarize and agree the next steps concerning your involvement – key actions and responsibilities before your next meeting. In most cases this will mean you presenting initial terms of reference for discussion

● Agree a date, time and place for your next meeting

- Agree a basis of maintaining regular contact and access to your client. For example:
  - Weekly 30-minute meeting to review progress
  - One page summary of key actions to be sent to your client every week
  - Monthly review meeting with your client and the project team
- Agree a form of communications with your client to announce your involvement on the project. Agree a distribution list of interested parties. Offer to draft this letter for your client to review and then circulate

INSIGHT

Watch out for the disappearing client syndrome! **At an initial meeting, you must discuss and agree with your client the communications and reporting arrangements for the proposed project. Often on projects consultants fall victim to the client who is promoted, becomes too busy or simply loses interest in a project. In effect, they disappear! So you must establish a basis for regular client access**

If you have, at your initial meeting, agreed precise reporting arrangements and subsequently confirmed these in your written proposal, you can refer to them if your client starts to miss review meetings. Regular client access allows you to update them on progress and problem areas. It also means you can do this sooner rather than later. You must always keep focused on your main client and not allow them to drift away from a project.

- Keep a record of your meeting

Write to your client confirming what was discussed and any agreed action points. Also confirm the date, time and place of your next meeting.

Things to avoid at initial meetings

Appearing unprepared or unprofessional is probably the worst impression to give any potential client at an initial meeting. Below is a list containing some classic errors. Avoid them at all costs.

- Not listening
- Talking too much at your client

- Not stating your objectives for the meeting
- Displaying arrogant or aggressive behaviour
- Running out of time to deal with all the issues
- Being drawn into making personal comments about other people or departments in your organization
- Voicing recommendations too early – remember, it may not be a systems or people issue
- Demonstrating a lack of confidence or credibility
- Leaving the meeting with the wrong problem
- Not being proactive enough in suggesting how events should progress to the next stage.

How to convey respect, openness and understanding at an initial client meeting

Respect

- Arrive on time
- Be polite and courteous
- Acknowledge your client's opinions and respect their values
- Agree a contract for your meeting
- Give your clients choice and decision making power during your meeting
- Allow your client time to talk about their concerns
- Give your client your full attention
- Avoid patronizing comments or observations.

Openness

- Be clear and open about your objectives
- Avoid matters which may involve organizational politics or intrigue
- Be prepared to admit any errors, mistakes or misunderstandings on your part
- Be honest about explaining the scope and limitations of your work

- Be honest in your answers – if you don't know, then say you don't know
- Challenge your client if you do not understand anything. It is better to ask earlier than later. Asking later may make you look foolish.

Understanding

- Demonstrate a real appreciation of your client's position
- Regularly summarize your client's answers and comments
- Ask for regular feedback from your clients on your work
- Remember that clients have feelings on issues.

INITIAL CLIENT MEETINGS CONSULTANT'S TEMPLATE

As part of your professional approach, you should always attend an initial meeting with your thoughts and questions prepared well in advance. This will ensure that you appear confident and knowledgeable. Equally, at the end of an initial meeting you need to record carefully the results of your client discussions. You should use the template at the end of this chapter to act as a focus for your questions and to record key points. Figures 3.3 and 3.4 provide some simple examples to illustrate how they might be used.

INITIAL TERMS OF REFERENCE

Why prepare initial terms of reference?

The most visible way in which you demonstrate to your client that you have understood their problem and requirements is by writing initial terms of reference. This document serves as the 'contract' between you and your client, and will be referenced and updated several times during the life of an assignment or project. In some cases even the main objectives may change, and these changes must be documented in

INITIAL MEETING FORM

Date/Time 3 March, 14:00	**Location** Head Office, NY

Dept Name/Present   Operations – John Hills, Mark Thomas

Meeting Purpose   To discuss the possibility of managing the merger of two production plants in New Jersey following an acquisition by PlayNow Toys Inc of Plastic Parts Inc, a plastic moulding company

What is the client reporting structure?	**Description of client's operation**
Jane Barns (CEO) John Mills (VP Prod) Alan Hall (Mngr) George Malvich (Mngr)	PlayNow Toys manufactures a variety of wooden and plastic toys for the US market, with an annual turnover of US $50m

What are your client's issues?	**Initial thoughts to solve problem**
Requirement to merge two factories following an acquisition. Each has different cultures and work processes Need to rationalize the workforce in wooden toys due to reduction in demand	Meet staff and understand differences in management styles. Review corporate goals. Develop an integration strategy Review demand figures. Look at export markets. Develop staff release scheme

Action	**Next meeting date/time/place**
Visit sites – JH, MT Interview key staff – MT Prepare integration strategy – MT	25 March, 10:00, Head Office, NY **Duration of meeting** 2 hours

Figure 3.3   *Initial client meetings – Example 1*

INITIAL MEETING FORM

Date/Time 12 Sept, 8 am	**Location** West End Office, London

Dept Name/Present   IT Dept – Sue Gates, Geoffrey Pitts, Sam Elbeik

Meeting Purpose   To discuss the possibility of migrating a reference database from a stand-alone computer to a small network of office workers

What is the client reporting structure?	**Description of client's operation**
Geoffrey Pitts (IT Director) Sue Gates (Supervisor) Roberta Small James Lock Tom Fry	IT Dept at Aircraft Data gathers and supplies information on both current and past flying machines including civil and military aircraft. Offices in London and Moscow

What are your client's issues?	**Initial thoughts to solve problem**
Current data are stored on a stand-alone PC. Want to network PCs	Look at cabling in building. Can we use existing kit? Buy new kit? Size of LAN? Location of users? Software licences?
Want to switch data access from proprietary language to Windows	Look at data size and structure. Windows preferred, use Access. Menu system? End user reports. Data input
Data in London and Moscow must be the same	Write program to automate the compare and update of data sets daily

Action	**Next meeting date/time/place**
Get budget – GP Detailed requirements meet – SE, SG Visit Moscow site with GP – SE, GP	18 Sept, 8 am, Moscow Office **Duration of meeting** 1.5 hours

Figure 3.4   *Initial client meetings – Example 2*

your initial terms of reference so that the focus for the project is not lost. It is essential that any changes to your initial terms of reference are discussed in detail and agreed by your client before they are implemented. No consultant has the power to change initial terms of reference without the express agreement of their client, and only when they have been approved by the client can a project truly begin.

What should the initial terms of reference contain?

The key characteristics of terms of reference is that they should be clear and concise. They must focus on your client's issues and, as such, will be based on your initial client meeting. You must indicate clearly what the project's objectives are and what you are proposing to do. You also need to highlight any constraints or assumptions you are making and show the key stages and milestones involved in your planned results. You will also have to indicate your costs and resourcing requirements. Use the template in the toolkit chapter at the end of this book to prepare your initial terms of reference. The headings to use and a description of their content include the following.

Background

- A description of the background to the work that needs to be done
- Identify any past problems or other relevant issues
- Include information gained from your initial client meeting
- Keep this section to a maximum of two paragraphs.

Objectives

- State the business objectives that must be achieved
- State who your client is.

Boundary

Document the boundaries or scope of the work to be covered. Clearly identify:

- what will be done
- what will not be done
- what departments will be involved.

Constraints

Record the constraints that you are working with, including:

- time
- people
- money
- equipment
- other resources.

Assumptions

- State the assumptions you are making, (for example, access to resources, client staff, financial budgets). This will indicate to your client what further information you will need
- When your initial terms of reference are signed off, there should be no assumptions in it, as you will have agreed or adjusted the basis on which you have agreed to carry out the work following your client discussions.

Client reporting

State the client reporting requirements, showing:

- who on the client side will receive your reports
- how these reports will be presented (meetings, electronic mail or paper)
- when the reports will be delivered.

Project deliverables

State the project deliverables, indicating:

- what the deliverables will be
- when they will be delivered
- note these down as milestones.

Activity time chart

- Show the major tasks involved in your project and their sequence
- Indicate when they will be done. Show the week number and completion dates
- Indicate how long they will take
- Show who will be completing these tasks
- Show the milestones where key deliverables will be made, e.g. presentation, report, system specification, operating procedures, client workshops.

Finance

- Show the fee rate for each resource
- Show the total estimated budget required.

Sample initial terms of reference

Our initial terms of reference headings have been transferred onto a form that you can use for your project. This form can be found in our chapter on the internal consultant toolkit. Review the example shown in Figure 3.5 which uses this form and consider how you might incorporate this approach in your consulting work.

Remember, at this stage you are preparing *initial* terms of reference based on your understanding of the project so far. These will change, and more detail will be added as the project progresses through the next two stages of understanding and defining your client problems and action planning. Even during the implementation stage your terms of reference may change.

CLIENT PROPOSALS

For some projects, you may be required to bid for the work you propose to carry out, and in such circumstances you will need to present a more formal document to your potential client. So you will need to expand your initial terms of reference into a full pro-

TERMS OF REFERENCE FORM - Page 1 of 3

Client Name Boris Lang	**Date** 16 August
Consultant Name Emily Goodson	**Location** Hamburg
Project Name Internal Support Department	**Start Date** 18 September

Background

- In the last two years, the Hamburg office has increased its staff from 30 to over 120. IT support for training and computer maintenance is currently supplied by two external companies. Service levels vary considerably

- Head office has an international drive to create internal IT support sections wherever possible throughout the company to provide greater control and quality of service to our employees

Objective

- To investigate the service level provided by the two external companies
- To document the skills required for an IT support function

Boundary

- Involve the senior management at Hamburg site
- Understand and document the services required
- Interview staff of external support company
- Interview staff at Hamburg site
- Determine level of satisfaction of employees
- Do not recommend individual employees for new post

Figure 3.5   *Terms of reference form*

TERMS OF REFERENCE FORM - Page 2 of 3

Constraints

- Details of this assignment must not be discussed with the external IT support companies

Assumptions

- Members of external IT support companies are available for interview
- Internal staff members are available for interview
- All interviewees will be available over a one-week period

Reporting

- Provide a brief progress report every Friday by 14:00
- Use the internal electronic mail system

Deliverables and milestones

- Provide a final report at the end of the assignment in four weeks' time
- Present the findings to the Personnel Director in New York

TERMS OF REFERENCE FORM - Page 3 of 3

Activity Time Chart for Project

Activity	Who	Effort	Start	Week 1 2 3 4 5 6 7 8
1. Prepare plan	EG	0.5		***
	BL	0.5		**
2. Services needed	EG	3		****
3. Investigate Co 1	EG	2		****
4. Investigate Co 2	EG	2		****
5. Interview staff	EG	4		*****
6. Report	EG	2		****
7. Presentation	EG	0.5		
	BL	0.5		

TOTAL Effort: 15 days

Estimated Costs

Resource Name: Emily Goodson	**Rate:** 900	**Effort:** 14	**Cost:** 12,600
Resource Name: Boris Lang	**Rate:** 1,500	**Effort:** 1	**Cost:** 1,500
Resource Name:	**Rate:**	**Effort:**	**Cost:**
Resource Name:	**Rate:**	**Effort:**	**Cost:**
Equipment Name:			**Cost:**
Equipment Name:			**Cost:**
Expenses:			**Cost:** 1,000

Total Estimated Costs: 15,000

Approved by Client: _____

Date: _____

posal. To do this, you have to include all the sections covered in your initial terms of reference and then add some further sections to enhance and complete your final proposal document.

Structure your proposal in a logical manner, and where there are several clients involved in the final decision-making process try to identify those who will have a key influence concerning the acceptance or rejection of your proposal. If at all possible, try to focus your marketing activities on these individuals so as to increase your chances of success.

INSIGHT

Keep the time spent on drafting your proposal in line with the size of the assignment on offer. Do not spend a week writing a proposal for a project that is likely to last a few days. You need to use your time effectively and focus your energies on proposals that offer best promise.

In special situations you may have to consider to what extent you can accept responsibility for the quality of work of third party contractors or consultants who may become involved in a project. You have to be conscious of your possible exposure in the event that a third party fails to complete their work on time. In such instances your proposal should specify your conditions for managing and accepting the involvement of other parties over whom you have no real control but whose work will impact on your work plan. Failure to deal with this type of issue can have disastrous consequences at a later date. Remember, the whole basis of effective client management is to avoid possible problems by predicting them in advance and then taking corrective action to ensure that they do not arise. This is what we mean by proactive client management, and the golden rule is never to surprise your client.

Submit your proposal to your client as a typed and narrative document. It must not be presented as a completed form. Use the same headings as in your initial terms of reference, but expand each section to provide more detailed information. For example:

- Enhance the boundary section by explaining the type of research or information gathering you will undertake, who you will want to interview and how much time you will need to complete the work
- Enhance the activity time chart by providing a description for each activity – indicating not only your responsibilities but also your client's
- Specify the time and costs involved and the use of other internal/external consultants. Remember to take into account factors such as holidays and the availability of clients and their staff. Agree any absences in advance with your client so as to avoid problems at a later stage
- Finally, remember to check all your key facts and numbers.

Additional headings you need to include in your proposal are as follows.

Consulting experience

This section outlines your professional expertise and competence to carry out the assignment. Include your previous experience in addressing similar projects or problems and also include your curriculum vitae. If you have a team that will be used for the project, include the details of your team's skills and experience.

Methodology

This section deals with your approach to tackling the project by describing in detail your approach or methodology. If you are involved in information technology or training consultancy, you might describe the process for conducting your development cycle (linear or iterative) or training needs analysis.

GETTING IN AND CONTRACTING WITH YOUR CLIENT: BEING CLIENT FOCUSED

The first stage in the internal consulting process involves establishing an initial working relationship with your client. The primary objective is for you to clearly identify your client's needs and then to begin exploring how you might provide assistance. It involves submitting terms of reference and agreeing in detail a project's objectives, time scales and costs.

Questions you should ask

- Does the client fully understand that they have a problem?
- Has your client identified the right or wrong problem?
- Does your client want to take full ownership of the problem?
- Is the client aware of their limitations in trying to solve the problem?
- Does your client see you as a partner in tackling the problem?
- Are there other important parties or clients who may need to be brought into the project to ensure a successful outcome?
- Is your client fully aware of their commitments and responsibilities in commissioning the project?
- What is the real problem facing your client?

Client's perspective of you

- Are you competent?
- Do you appear professional?
- Can I work with you and trust you?
- Do you have the right expertise and track record?
- Are your initial thoughts and plan practical and realistic?
- Are your terms of reference or proposal reasonable?

Other client thoughts

▶ Do you report to other senior people in the organization?

▶ Are you arrogant?

▶ Do you value my time?

Other statements/questions you might use

▶ What are the real issues as you see them?

▶ If we were successful, what would success look like?

▶ What role do you see us playing in helping you to address the problem?

▶ Why have you asked us to provide some assistance?

▶ Have you considered these other options . . .?

▶ What are your main business concerns at the moment?

▶ What will happen if the situation continues?

▶ What have other people said about the situation?

▶ Could we have access to those reports, that data?

▶ Are there any parts of the organization or areas that you do not want us to get involved in?

▶ What do your colleagues think about the situation?

▶ These are our initial thoughts about tackling the work . . .

4 Understanding and defining your client's problem

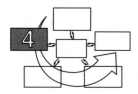

UNDERSTANDING AND DEFINING YOUR CLIENT'S PROBLEM

The first step, after having had your initial terms of reference or proposal agreed and accepted by your client, is to begin understanding in detail your client's problem. This requires an analytical review of the issues or circumstances surrounding a particular problem. In defining your client's problem, you need to maintain at all times a clear and independent perspective. You must not allow yourself to be easily persuaded by emotive arguments or persuasive people. Maintaining an objective outlook is essential.

In understanding your client's problem, you will need to gather information from a variety of individuals and sources. This information is normally collected through five key methods:

- Desk research
- Interviews
- Group interviews
- Questionnaires
- Process mapping.

In this chapter we explore the essential elements of these approaches and provide some key advice on how to utilize them to secure maximum benefit in your client projects. Two key factors that will help you determine the most appropriate approach to use are the number of people you can reasonably expect to involve given your time constraints and the depth of knowledge you need to understand the problem fully. Figure 4.1 illustrates the relationship of these two factors to the different approaches.

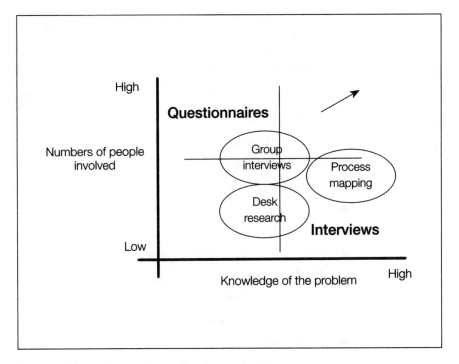

Figure 4.1   *Information gathering techniques*

DESK RESEARCH

In most cases you will carry out desk research in the early stages of a project, although there may be circumstances where it will be triggered during the middle of a project. Desk research involves the identification and analysis of specific sources of documentary evidence that may be relevant to your consulting project. Of course, there may be lots of projects where desk research is limited to reading up on some background papers. But there may be other times where you will need to access lots of different sources of information in preparation for the start of a project. In such cases you will need to apply a disciplined and analytical approach to your work so as to identify the relevant sources of information and record the salient points for your consultancy project.

Desk research normally involves three stages:

● Identification of relevant sources of information

- Review and analysis of the information sources
- Preparation of key findings and conclusions resulting from the research.

It might involve reviewing the following sources of information:

- Organization reports
- Procedures and operating manuals
- Competitor publications
- Financial reports
- Technical journals
- Professional association reports and journals
- Trade journals
- Specialist journals
- Business magazines
- Government reports
- Consultancy surveys and reports
- Industry association reports
- Relevant books.

Desk research helps build up your understanding of a particular issue and will usually result in you producing a report highlighting your key findings.

INTERVIEWING CLIENTS

'I listen, listen, listen – a lot.'
Peter Fraser, Group Human Resources Consultant, Zurich Australian Insurance Group

Preparing your interview structure

The first point to emphasize when interviewing people during the course of any project or assignment is that everyone either is or has the' potential to become a client. You must therefore always conduct yourself with the utmost courtesy and professionalism, even when interviewing people who may be unhelpful or even impolite. As an internal consultant, you cannot predict when you might end up working for someone on another project. So you must always exercise care when conducting interviews. Treat everyone with equal respect.

An interview is a technique for gaining information through questioning and discussion. Any client interview must be controlled by the consultant and have a clear set of objectives. At the same time, your interview must not give the impression of being an interrogation, as that will antagonize people and result in a negative outcome. As the consultant, it is also your responsibility not to allow any personality conflicts or extraneous issues to cloud your judgement during an interview.

In preparing for interviews, you must develop a checklist of all the issues you want to discuss. A broad set of questions will tend to be more helpful than a detailed list, as the questions you will ultimately ask will depend on the replies and reactions you receive as the interview progresses. You therefore need to be flexible in your approach, and a checklist provides you with more scope to adjust the focus and flow of your interview in response to client responses.

The key objective of any interview is to get your client talking. Again, try to use the 80:20 Pareto rule, with your client speaking for 80 per cent of the time and you asking questions for the remaining 20 per cent. If you dominate an interview, it is likely that you will leave it not having understood your client's viewpoint or, even worse, their problem. Your ability to listen rather than talk is critical. The most successful client interviews are those where you simply use a small but select number of open-ended questions and your client provides all the relevant information. A bad interview is where you do all the talking.

Your behaviour during the initial stages will tend to determine the level of trust that will exist throughout the interview. You therefore need to display lots of interest and empathy with your client. You can accelerate this process by offering to share control of the interview, displaying openness in your objectives and jointly agreeing the agenda.

At the beginning of every interview you will need to establish your credibility as well as deal with any anxieties your client may have about the process. Appearing worried or nervous yourself can sometimes arouse similar tensions in your client. At the introduction stage of the interview you do not need to present a highly detailed explanation of your technical qualifications and career details, as this can be interpreted by some clients as demonstrating a lack of confidence or, even worse, arrogance. Your objective is to instil in your client a sense of comfort and mutual respect, so you should simply state who you are, your role, some general background to the interview and your objectives for the meeting.

In developing and planning your approach to interviews, try to keep to the following guidelines:

- Analyse in advance any background information on your client's operation, e.g. problem areas, performance indicators, key personalities, current business challenges, competitor threats
- State clearly your aims and objectives for the interview
- Decide on the topics you want to focus on, preferably with the aid of a checklist
- Prepare and then plan your interview structure
- Allocate timings for each section of your interview
- Find out and agree with your client where the interview will take place. As a general rule, people are more comfortable in their own surroundings. They will also have easy access to any additional information you may require
- When making any interview appointment with clients, always confirm the purpose and objectives of the meeting. Ideally, write to them in advance to confirm these details and enclose a draft agenda. This helps to allay any concerns they may have

about the interview and helps prepare them to deal with the questions and issues you want to discuss. You will then be able to refer to the agenda and use it as a means of controlling the pace of your interview

- If you are interviewing with a colleague, make sure that you agree clear roles beforehand and allocate questions or specific topic areas to each other. You must give your client a professional impression and show that you both have strong roles in the project. Having one consultant not asking any questions for an entire interview does not instil client confidence. Even worse, it could give the impression that you are wasteful and inefficient

- Try to ensure or agree with your client that there will be no interruptions.

INSIGHT

As internal consultants, always try to 'hunt in pairs'. Interviewing a client alone can be difficult, as it is very easy to get locked into a pattern of discussion and not realize that you have lost track or control. By working with another colleague you can develop specific roles and help each other if one of you starts getting into difficulties.

Managing your client interview

'I try to avoid making judgements about people particularly in public. Always try to deal with the issue not the person.'

  Peter Fraser, Group Human Resources Consultant, Zurich Australian Insurance Group

At the start of any interview you must outline the purpose of the interview and check again the inter- viewee's understanding of the objectives. Even if you have previously sent a written confirmation to a client, it may be the case that they did not read it properly or that they have forgotten about it. After having indi- cated the time you require for the interview, you should politely request the assistance and agreement of the interviewee to your objectives. You should also ask your client whether they wish to add anything to the interview agenda. These formal courtesies help overcome any potential hostility that might surround a project.

Your questioning technique should allow your client to follow their own line of thought provided they do not move too far away from the areas you want to focus on. However, you will need to be conscious of any time constraints that you and your client may be working under. You should also remember that people are likely to disclose more when they feel comfortable and free to express themselves. Adopting an aggressive questioning stance is not necessary and will only result in your interviewee becoming antagonized and refusing to offer any real information. Also try to avoid interrupting or being overly critical of anything they may say. You may need to challenge them on some points, but you can do this without adopting a hostile questioning technique.

At the end of the interview you should summarize what your client has stated and thank them for their help and co-operation. You should also request permission to come back to them for additional information should your work require it.

INSIGHT

A professional way to end a client interview is to ask your client whether there is anything that you have not discussed or raised that they think may be relevant to the work you are undertaking. In most cases you will get a neutral response, but on some occasions you will get a really important piece of information that will help your overall project. Equally, this question has the desired effect of handing over the close of the interview to your client.

Managing client interviews: a checklist

- Make your client feel comfortable and at ease
- Ensure that your client is clear about the objectives for the interview
- Obtain your client's agreement to your objectives and allow them to add to them
- Ask for permission to take notes during the interview

- State how you intend to handle issues of confidentiality – being open and honest will help you establish rapport and trust
- Outline what will happen with the information you are collecting
- Encourage your client to do most of the talking
- Use open-ended questions at the beginning of the interview
- Follow up client answers by using probing questions which elicit more details about issues
- Confirm your understanding of what has been said by summarizing regularly
- Try not to be drawn into making specific comments on controversial issues and do not align yourself to any one viewpoint
- Never criticize other people or departments.

Also don't forget to:

- keep on track with your interview structure
- ensure that all your topic areas are covered
- ask for information on any new issues that emerge during the interview
- obtain specific examples, details or facts of what your client is trying to explain
- recognize irritation on the part of your client
- thank your interviewee for their time and assistance
- advise them about what will happen next.

Things to avoid during information gathering interviews

- Talking too much at your client
- Unnecessary jargon – it irritates clients and provides some with a ready opportunity to criticize you or your work; if not during the interview then almost certainly later with their colleagues
- Interrupting your client
- Making assumptions about the interviewee's views

or opinions – check out or challenge all assumptions
- Asking leading or multiple questions
- Antagonizing your client through aggressive behaviour
- Running out of time.

Taking interview notes

Information which is obtained in the course of any interview should be recorded during the interview. Most consultants have to work hard at improving the quality of their note taking. It can be a difficult task to take precise and detailed notes during a lengthy interview, and you will need to develop a disciplined approach so as not to end up with pages of scribbled and semi-intelligible comments.

First, you must record the name and role of the interviewee and the date on which the interview took place. At first this sounds obvious, but again it is amazing how, after you have interviewed perhaps twenty-five people, you look at a set of notes and wonder whose comments they belong to. The combined use of your broad list of questions and topic headings should assist you in structuring the information as the interview proceeds.

You will also need to subsequently review the information you obtain to check that it provides you with what you require to carry out your investigation or research. Clearly, the disciplined and analytical approach involved in collecting information is equally necessary in recording it.

INSIGHT

When your client is discussing sensitive information it pays to be careful in how you take notes. Making copious notes as your client reveals their innermost thoughts about the organization's problems or politics will not induce a sense of comfort. Try to listen and then make notes after the discussion has moved away from the delicate information. This will get over the problem of your client feeling that you are some kind of policeman.

Actions to take after an interview

- Write up a full account of the interview as soon as possible

- Send a copy of your interview notes to the interviewee so that they can check and correct any misunderstandings or, alternatively, add any relevant points that may have been missed. This makes for clear communications and also presents a thorough and professional image.

GROUP INTERVIEWS

Group interviews involve situations where, for efficiency or operational concerns, you decide to interview a group of people regarding issues involving your project. In some situations you may be faced with a group of production workers taking an extended lunch break to accommodate your project schedule. Alternatively, you may be asked to interview a group of managers at the end of one of their regular review meetings. In many respects, the basic requirements of handling these types of interviews are the same as for one-to-one situations.

However, you do need to be aware that in certain circumstances there may be requirements to ensure that everyone has an equal contribution and that the discussions are not dominated by the more forceful members of the group. To that extent, you may need to exercise strong control. One way that you can do this is to introduce the concept of groundrules to guide people's behaviour during the discussions. Some simple but powerful examples are included in Figure 4.2 below.

Using structured frameworks to obtain information

In group situations involving larger groups of, say twelve or more people, you may consider introducing some structured group work to solicit everyone's views. To do this, you might break up the group into smaller

- **Only one person speaks at a time** A basic discipline, but one that often needs to be enforced in group situations to avoid several discussions taking place at once

- **People can agree to disagree** This helps you move the discussion forward if it appears to be getting bogged down between a minority of participants

- **It is OK to be negative but also try to offer positive alternative solutions or ideas to address the problem** This can help you manage people to be positive in their attitude. In some situations a group interview can degenerate into a negative spiral unless it is properly managed

- **Hierarchy is left at the door** This can be helpful if you are having to manage a cross-section of people and believe that there may be concerns about status influencing people's views

- **Let's be hard on the issue and soft on the people** This rule helps you focus people on getting to issues concerning problem areas rather than allowing personal recriminations to take place, which can often happen in heated situations

As the consultant, you will need to introduce these groundrules at the outset of your group meeting and state that they are there to help ensure a productive exchange of views. Having introduced them, it is essential that you then police them during the meeting in order to derive the real benefit

Figure 4.2 *Groundrules for controlling group interviews*

groups of four or six people and task them with discussing a set of specific questions and reporting back. In this type of situation you might typically use the classic SWOT analysis which requires a review of the strengths, weaknesses, opportunities and threats of a particular situation. Figure 4.3 illustrates this framework.

After having introduced the framework, you would instruct small groups of people to spend 20–30 minutes producing their SWOT analysis on how they viewed a specific problem or situation. As the internal consultant, you would then ask someone from each group to present their analysis and lead a discussion to clarify your understanding of what is being presented. Once a SWOT analysis has been presented, you can use some of the additional dimensions as shown in Figure 4.3 to promote further discussion, e.g. What is the risk and severity of that actually happening?

Another analytical tool that you can use very easily in a group interview situation is the force-field analysis. This requires you to highlight a particular problem or objective and then to get people to brainstorm or relate their experiences to the issue. In using the framework, you have to direct people's thoughts and discussions into two distinct areas. The driving or forcing factors are those that people being interviewed believe are capable of solving the problem or achieving the objective. In contrast, the blockers or obstacles are those factors that people believe are preventing the

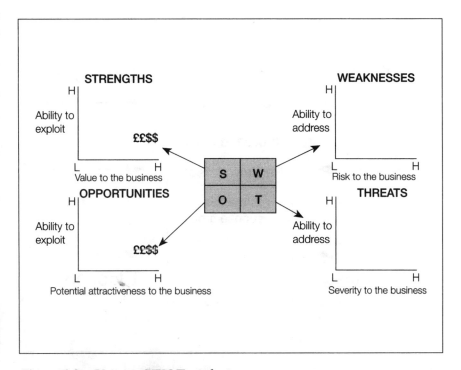

Figure 4.3   Using a SWOT analysis

problem from being addressed or the objective achieved. When structuring these exercises you should provide people with flip-charts, as part of their power is their ability to visually display a lot of potentially complex information. Figure 4.4 provides a simple outline of the forcefield approach.

The benefits of both these frameworks are that they enable people to present their views and opinions in a structured and focused way. This helps both them and you, as you are able to collect information in an efficient and controlled manner. You also have an effective means of recording the outcomes of these meetings, as each group will have presented their views on flip-chart paper which means that they can easily be typed up and edited after the meeting. These frameworks are also simple to explain and highly participative, which is essential to getting the best out of any group interview situation.

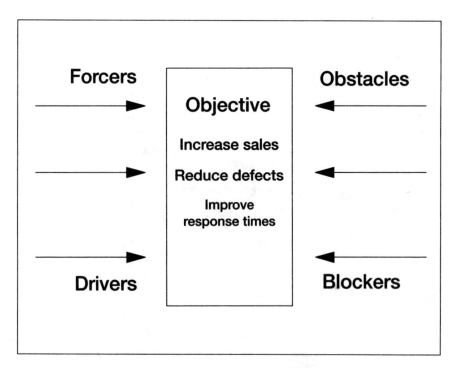

Figure 4.4 *Using a force-field analysis*

TYPES OF INTERVIEW QUESTIONING TECHNIQUES

Developing a professional interview technique is crucial to gathering information and building rapport with your clients. With your overall interview objectives already clear there are several types of questioning technique you can use to help you collect information. But at the outset of any interview consider whether you are trying to:

- obtain hard facts
- clarify your understanding of a process, issue or problem
- get your interviewee to comment on an idea or proposition
- challenge your interviewee's thinking
- understand the attitudes and feelings surrounding an issue
- assess the interviewee.

Once you have decided on these aims, you can then employ a whole range of questioning techniques and devices. Developing ease with these questions and techniques will come naturally as you gain more experience of interviewing people. In the early days of your consulting work you should try to experiment with these techniques and not be too worried if on certain occasions they do not always produce the desired result. Interviewing is a skill that develops over a period of time.

Using open-ended questions

Open-ended questions are an essential element in any consultant's interview toolkit, as they prevent your client from giving simple one-word replies. Open-ended questions encourage people to talk, and are particularly helpful during the initial stages of an interview as they promote positive rapport and dialogue. The most powerful open-ended questions begin with the words: **What, Why, When, How, Where and Who**. Open-ended questions are also a highly effective way of either introducing new topics into an interview or of probing for more detailed information on a particular subject.

Examples of open-ended questions

What was actually happening at that point?
How would you describe the current situation?
What are the current facts as regards service levels?
What are the performance figures relating to the system?
What were the precise objections raised by the customer?
Where is the unit at this present point in time?
When was the discrepancy first identified?
What do you see as the three major issues facing your operation?
Why did that situation remain unchanged for so long?
How are the current systems managed?
How would you describe the current strengths of the operation?
Who had the primary responsibility?
When did the situation begin to worsen?
When did management realize that the project was beginning to slip?
What other issues have contributed to the problem?
When did you realize that customers were reacting badly?
What would 'Y' be expected to do in such situations?

Open-ended questions can also be used to understand your clients' views and opinions on specific issues, e.g.:

How do you feel about. . .?
What do you think about. . .?
What do you think of the idea that. . .?
What are your views on. . .?
How important are . . . would you say?
What alternatives are available?
How would you react if. . .?

Using specific questions

Specific questions allow you to probe for and obtain specific details or facts surrounding an issue. In many cases you want to emerge from an interview with lots of hard facts and not just opinions. Specific questions help you to get the details. You should use them to follow up on open-ended questions. Some examples are:

When exactly did that situation first arise?
Who is responsible for or owns that process?
When did the breakdown first happen?
Why did the operator report the incident to you first?
What were the exact circumstances involved?
What was the agreed conclusion to those discussions?
What was the percentage increase at that time?
How was the report presented to the management?
Did anyone query the specification the first time it was announced?

Linking questions

The link question is a variation of the open-ended question. It acts as a bridge and allows you to make a transition from one question to another, thus promoting a smooth interview flow. Examples of link questions include:

You mentioned just now that. . . . How did this affect. . .?
We've just discussed. . . . Could we now have a look at. . .?
How does that issue relate to the point you raised earlier concerning. . .?
Is there a relationship between x and y?
As you finished talking about product x, it brings to mind some questions I have that relate to product y. How strong a product is that?

Exploring alternative approaches with your client

During certain interviews, and more particularly during the later stages of a project, you may need to begin validating certain hypotheses, strategies or actions. Using the following types of questions can help you obtain reactions from interested parties or clients. The skill is to suggest the idea or proposition, but not sound as though you have already reached a conclusion as this may discourage your client from giving a clear and unbiased answer. You want your client to give you a straightforward reaction to the proposition or proposal.

Perhaps we could do it another way, such as. . .?
Is this the only option available? What about the xy approach? Would that work?
What about taking a radically different approach, such as. . .?
Can we look at it this way. . . . How about integrating all the activities together?
Next time could we complete the job using. . .?
What if your competitors did the opposite and started pursuing the idea – would that suggest it could be made to work?
I am told that with sufficient resources the process can produce those results – what are your thoughts?

Providing non-verbal encouragement during interviews

Non-verbal encouragement involves you in making comments such as: 'Ah', 'Oh?', 'Uhh?', 'Hmm' as your client talks. This is a rapport-building technique which lets your client know that you are actively listening and that you would like to hear more. Verbal acknowledgements are indications of attention and when combined with appropriate facial expressions (smiles, raised eyebrows, etc.), they further encourage your client to talk. You can also show empathy to your client by the careful use of body posture, facial expressions and eye contact. Leaning forward and making expressions of interest can promote real dialogue. However, be careful not to overplay these techniques as some clients may find them manipulative.

Using supportive statements

Supportive statements involve phrases such as: 'I see ...', 'And then what happened?', 'That's interesting'. They produce the same results as non-verbal encouragement – an extended answer from your client which reduces the need for a set of further detailed questions from you. The aim in using supportive statements is to lead your client into providing as much information and detail as possible with the least amount of spoken comment from you as the consultant.

Checking your facts

Throughout any assignment and during any interview you may need to establish specific facts or request key information. This requires a more direct approach to asking questions, but you need to exercise care to ensure that you do not sound hostile towards people. The directness of the question sometimes makes this difficult, so you need to consider your voice tone, the sensitivity of the question and the most appropriate timing of it during your interview. The following types of question illustrate the approach:

Where did that information come from?
Can you confirm those figures?
Can you confirm that you do actually report to the Operations Director?
I have been shown a separate set of figures on. . . .
Can you confirm their accuracy?
So what is the current system's availability?
Can you verify this data?

Showing empathy with your client

At certain times you will need to demonstrate empathy with your client. This can be particularly important when your client is discussing sensitive issues and feeling vulnerable about relating particular details. The following statements can help you to get through these difficult areas of an interview:

You are really concerned about this, aren't you?
I can see this has caused you a great deal of concern.
It is pretty obvious from what you have said why you were annoyed.
I can understand how you must have felt about the situation.
That must have been a really difficult situation to deal with.

In other situations you may need to offer some kind of support or assistance to your client in order to engage their continued support and interest, in which case the following statements can be helpful:

Yes, it is irritating, but let me see if I can help.
You are quite right to be angry, but I can suggest some ideas for resolving the issue.
There is every reason to feel set up, but have you thought about. . . .
Can you tell me the details? I may be able to. . . .

Key word repetition

Key word repetition is another rapport building technique which encourages your client to offer more information on a particular issue that you may have under discussion. It simply requires you to pick up on a key word and reflect it back to your client in the following manner:

Client *'For two years I've been working on systems design.'*
Internal Consultant: *'Oh . . . systems design. . . .'*

When 'Oh . . . systems design' is phrased with a

questioning voice tone, this can often be sufficient to prompt your client to explain more about the subject. It is a technique which again allows you to interview someone with an economy of questions.

Using the pause

If you want your interviewee to continue talking and add to what he or she has already said, a strong pause can stimulate this as effectively as any spoken question. The judicious use of the pause is one of the most powerful techniques to employ in any interview, and you should develop a strong capability in using it. Immediately rushing in with another question to avoid any momentary silence can result in a client failing to offer an important piece of information.

A pause provides your interviewee with a chance to think, rephrase or add to any preceding answers. As Mark Twain once wrote:

'The right word may be effective but no word was ever as effective as a rightly timed pause.'

Using summaries

You should use summaries regularly throughout any interview. They allow you to check your understanding of any facts that you have been given and to clarify your client's thoughts on important issues. Summary statements also provide you with another method of achieving a smooth change of direction from one topic to another during your interview.

Summary questions prevent your client from drifting away from your interview agenda and allow you to regain control without an abrupt interruption. To that extent, they are very helpful in controlling talkative clients.

Summary statements involve phrases such as:

As I have understood the situation, what you are saying is that. . . .

So what you're saying is. . . . Is that correct?
If I have understood you correctly. . . . Now could we move on to discuss. . . .

Dealing with errors during an interview

Occasionally as a consultant you must expect to make a mistake about some issue or information during the course of an interview. The best advice is to openly admit to your client that you have made a mistake, offer an apology and move on. Trying to cover up the issue or avoid it will only make things worse. So if this happens, try using the following statements:

Sorry, that is my mistake!
You're right, I got it wrong. I do apologize.
That's quite right, I should have realized. . . . Please accept my apologies.
I apologize for misunderstanding that particular issue.

Avoiding the use of counter-productive questions

Any question which detracts from the smooth dialogue and conduct of an interview might be called counter-productive. Examples include the following.

Multiple questions

Multiple questions combine several questions into one long statement. The result is to add confusion to the interview process and allow your interviewee to be selective in his or her answer. Invariably, clients fail to address all the questions that you posed.

So how did you manage to achieve those results without impacting on other parts of the operation, and how did your colleagues react?
Why did you join this part of the organization and how does it compare with the other operation that you worked in?
So how long have you worked in this operation, and do you like it or are there problems?

Leading questions

Another counter-productive question is the leading question, which either invites a particular response or suggests that a 'right' answer is required from your client. The leading question is often phrased in the form of an emotional appeal such as:

You've got to admit that. . . .
Isn't it a fact that. . .?
You must concede that. . . .
You will surely acknowledge. . .?
You're not suggesting that. . .?
You don't think that. . .?

In the case of some of the above examples, you may be expecting the answer, 'Yes, of course!' In others, the obviously appropriate answer is, 'No, of course not'. In either case you are suggesting to your client that you have an answer in mind and that you would like it confirmed. Of course, there are some circumstances where this might prove an effective technique to test out someone's views. But you must be careful.

Critical leading questions

The critical leading question relies for its effect on a degree of implied criticism:

Surely you can't believe that, can you?
You don't really think that, do you?
Surely you're not suggesting that. . .?
You don't honestly think that, do you?
You cannot for one minute believe your competition would ever do that, do you?

Any response other than a strong rejection of the question appears to imply a lack of credibility on the part of your client. The critical leading question can therefore frequently appear antagonistic and so, in some situations, provoke a negative client reaction. This type of question should be avoided unless you feel that your client relationship would not be harmed by such a direct question.

USING QUESTIONNAIRES TO GATHER INFORMATION

While interviews allow you to question people in depth on specific issues, questionnaires make it possible for you to assess the views of a large number of people relatively quickly and cheaply. Questionnaires can therefore be a very efficient and effective way of gathering information from a wide group of people. They can also introduce a degree of quantitative data into your analysis and so overcome later arguments about people's views. Questionnaires can be used on a wide range of projects involving staff and customer surveys, reactions to new information technology systems and other organizational improvements. So for any internal consultant, understanding the steps involved in designing and administering a questionnaire can be extremely useful.

While it is possible to develop a questionnaire without too much difficulty, there are some rules that you should observe. Figure 4.5 illustrates a broad overview of the questionnaire design process.

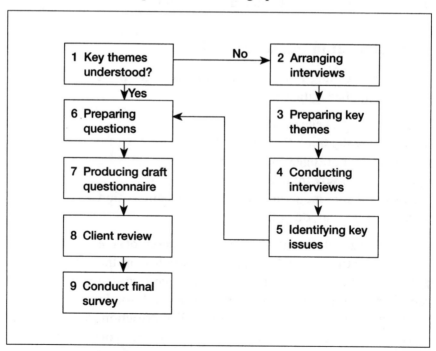

Figure 4.5 *Developing a questionnaire*

Designing a questionnaire

The process of designing a questionnaire can be divided into a series of nine key steps which involve the following:

- Step 1 – Identifying your questionnaire themes by interviewing people
- Step 2 – Arranging initial interviews
- Step 3 – Preparing key themes for your interviews
- Step 4 – Conducting interviews
- Step 5 – Identifying key issues
- Step 6 – Preparing and reviewing questions
- Step 7 – Producing your draft questionnaire
- Step 8 – Reviewing your draft questionnaire with your client
- Step 9 – Conducting the survey with your finalized questionnaire.

Step 1: Identifying your questionnaire themes by interviewing people

The first step in designing any questionnaire is to agree with your client the number of people who will be interviewed so that you can identify the key themes or issues to be included in your survey.

There are no specific rules as to the number of people that you should interview. But you will need to ensure that you include a cross-section of people who will ultimately appear in your final survey. This ensures that any views or issues which reflect different interest groups will emerge in your interviews and so find a place in your final questionnaire design.

One important decision that you will have to make is whether to interview people individually or in groups. Normally, senior managers prefer to be interviewed on their own, but it is also, of course, possible to interview people effectively in small groups. The group approach saves both time and money although, as we have discussed earlier, it can sometimes be operationally difficult to manage. You will need to discuss the various practical and operational implications of these approaches with your client before proceeding.

A further issue involves selecting the right people for your interviews. In our experience, it is better if you draw up a list of names and then discuss their suitability with your client. Because the people you select may not always be readily available you should agree a clear basis on which you can select alternatives. To save time, it is preferable to agree with your client that you can approach substitutes for interview without constantly having to refer back to them unless there are operational constraints. You will also need to ensure that your client provides a representative sample of people so that you get a balanced and realistic set of views and not just those that your client wants you to hear. So if in doubt, make sure that you challenge some of your client's decisions.

Step 2: Arranging initial interviews

You must compose and circulate a letter in advance of your interviews explaining the purpose and objectives of the exercise. Your letter should also detail the date, time and location of the interview and identify the topic areas you want to discuss. You should also thank people in advance for agreeing to participate in the exercise and express your wish to minimize any operational disturbance that your visit might bring. You should schedule interviews for between one and a half and two hours depending on the type of survey you are conducting and you should be able to hold between four and six interview sessions per day.

Step 3: Preparing key themes for your interviews

Before conducting your interviews, you will need to draw up a list of possible topics and issues for discussion. You will have already discussed and agreed these with your client in advance of any interview programme. As we stated in our interview section, this list of themes should only be used as an outline and prompt, rather than as a detailed checklist to be followed rigorously. It will then help provide a focus and structure to your interviews and ensure a smooth flow.

Step 4: Conducting interviews

During this stage you try to keep on schedule and hope that you do not experience any last-minute cancellations. You will also need to maintain your discipline in recording information during the interviews. Any spare time between interviews should be used to write up your interview notes and plan ahead.

Step 5: Identifying key issues

From your interview notes, you must then develop a summary of the issues raised by people. You need to document the location, department or function of the people involved and write a short paragraph describing the various issues raised. In many cases you will have confirmed the issues already identified during your earlier client discussions. You will, however, need to review these issues with your client when preparing the final questionnaire, as the chances are that new issues will have emerged. For example, you may have identified from your interviews three recurring themes, such as pay and rewards, staff morale and the restructuring plan. When you come to review these issues with your client, you may find that only two of these issues need to be dealt with in the survey as the third will be the subject of a separate review. The end result is that you would have two key issues from which to begin developing your questionnaire. Your next action is to begin to shape your questionnaire content by preparing a set of questions for each theme.

Step 6: Preparing and reviewing questions

The following is a checklist that will help you to prepare a set of questions. The most effective approach is to:

- prepare questions for each issue that was raised
- add additional questions based on any other research you may have conducted
- brainstorm as many other relevant questions as you can
- refine your list, deleting questions that appear irrelevant, repetitive or redundant. Reword others as appropriate. It is often necessary to draft questions three or four times before arriving at a final draft questionnaire
- check that you have the right balance of negative and positive questions
- make sure the questions are understandable. Keep them simple and clear
- make sure that people have the necessary knowledge or experience to answer the questions accurately.

Ask specific questions

General questions should not be used when specific answers are required. For example:

'Are you satisfied with IT Help Desk response?'

This is not a good question if what you really want to find out is how quickly the IT Help Desk responds when a phone call is made. So a better question to ask would be:

'The IT Help Desk picks up my phone call in less than three rings'.

Avoid ambiguous questions

Ambiguous questions allow people the opportunity to provide different interpretations to the same question, and so produce meaningless results. For example:

'Do you often work overtime because of lack of administrative support?'

If the answer to this question was 'No', then what does it actually mean?

'No, I do not often work overtime'
or
'No, I do not lack administrative support'.

You can see that questions like this leave you open to criticism at the feedback stage. So be clear about what it is you are trying to measure or assess.

Use precise wording

Words such as 'fairly', 'generally', 'often', 'many' and 'appropriate' should be avoided, as you will then tend to generate inconsistent responses from different people. What is 'fairly good support' for one person is 'poor support' to another.

Avoid leading questions

Questions should be presented in a neutral way so as to prevent the manipulation of a desired response. An example of a leading question is:

'Do you feel your hard work is appreciated?'

The way to avoid the inherent bias that this type of question can produce is to introduce a number of questions around the central theme of reward which can then be collectively analysed. For example:

'On average, I work more than 40 hours each week'.
'My salary is below the national average for the job I do'.
'My manager gives me praise when I do a good job'.

Leading questions can also be caused by a failure to state alternatives. For example:

'Do you prefer working for a manager of your own sex?'

instead of

'Would you rather work for a man or a woman, or doesn't it matter?'

Keep questions short

Long questions should be kept to a minimum, as they reduce the amount of time people need to spend completing the questionnaire and so any sense of irritation or possible misunderstanding on the part of the person completing the document.

Careful phrasing

Never ask a question that will put someone on the defensive or make him or her feel in the wrong. Questions that people find rude or inconsiderate may not only affect their reply but may also affect their response to the survey as a whole. Also, always remember to avoid jargon and abbreviations unless it is clear that people understand what they mean.

Step 7: Producing your draft questionnaire

Having prepared your questions, you will then need to begin the process of structuring your questionnaire format, and the first key issue to address is the response scale that you will use.

Response format: Likert Scale

The most favoured format to use for your questionnaire response is the Likert Scale. This involves asking people whether they agree or disagree with a statement by indicating on a scale their strength of agreement or disagreement. There are usually five basic responses:

- Strongly disagree
- Disagree
- Uncertain/No opinion/Don't know
- Agree
- Strongly agree.

There should be an equal number of alternating positive and negative worded questions in your questionnaire so as to avoid any potential bias. The advantage of a Likert Scale is that it measures the strength of an attitude or belief while at the same time is easy for people to complete.

Response format: Free-form replies

Free-form replies are open-ended questions which allow people to write what they want on a subject. However, you should avoid structuring the questionnaire so that a free-form reply is needed to answer each question. This is because:

- a significant amount of time is needed by people to answer these questions, and it is likely that this time and effort will reduce the overall response rate to your questionnaire. People will simply get fed up with writing or not bother at all
- those who write the most will inevitably exert more influence on the results
- collecting and analysing the responses is very time-consuming
- there are many difficulties in analysing and presenting the replies in a structured and systematic way, as people will tend to write what they want and you end up with lots of diverse

information which is difficult to present back to your client.

Final section

Free-form replies can yield useful information. So for many surveys it may be a good idea to include a section at the end of your questionnaire which invites people to add any comments without presenting a specific question for them to answer. This has the advantage of allowing people to raise issues which they feel strongly about and which have not been covered by the questionnaire. However, analysis of such data should be treated with caution, since it is likely that only a relatively small proportion of people will make additional comments and these will not necessarily be representative of the whole group being surveyed.

Nevertheless, you will generate some useful comments that you may find valuable in the client feedback stage.

Using checklist responses

Checklist responses are a good method to use where you need to collect responses to a question other than agreement or disagreement. An example of a checklist format is:

'I work the following hours on my computer each day:

☐ Less than 1 hour
☐ 1–3 hours
☐ More than 3 hours'

Number of questions

Your questionnaire should be no longer than is absolutely necessary to achieve its purpose. The temptation in questionnaire design is always to ask too many questions. Lengthy questionnaires are unlikely to be answered accurately or completely and in many situations an overly complex questionnaire will result in a low response rate. So keep things short and brief.

Demographic data (personal details)

To analyse people's responses and identify different views without breaking confidentiality, it is customary, on the front of your questionnaire, to ask people to categorize themselves according to their organization grade, location, department or any other item that you may have agreed with your client. You do, however, need to be careful that too detailed a breakdown will not lead people to suspect that their individual responses can be identified, as this might affect their replies.

Completion time and return

The amount of time someone should take to complete your questionnaire should be explained on the first page of the questionnaire as part of your general instructions. People should not be asked to complete a questionnaire in too short a period of time as this may mean that they will rush it and not give accurate responses.

With regard to returning the questionnaire after completion, you should set on average a target of ten working days from distribution to return. This should provide people with sufficient time and also give you time to manage the logistics surrounding the exercise. Avoid periods of longer than ten days as this indicates a lack of urgency and priority in people's minds and will result in a weaker response rate.

Questionnaire instructions

You must provide clear instructions on how to complete the questionnaire. Use bold print and block capitals to emphasize key points and:

- indicate how all the questions should be answered, for example, by circling, crossing or ticking the answers
- show what each category of response means, for example, 1 = Strongly agree, 5 = Strongly disagree

- tell people how to correct mistakes in their answers
- indicate the time it should take to complete the questionnaire
- remind people to complete the personal details section and check that they have answered all the questions before returning the questionnaire
- clearly state to whom they should return the questionnaire and by what date.

Covering letter

Before finalizing the content of your draft question- naire you should prepare a letter to accompany it. This should contain the following information:

- The purpose of the questionnaire
- Who has commissioned it
- Why the individual has been selected to complete the questionnaire
- The confidentiality agreements surrounding the results
- Explain that there is no right or wrong answer
- Explain what the next steps are
- Thank people in advance for their co-operation.

Ideally, this letter should be either signed off by you or your client. In highly sensitive projects it may be better for you as the consultant to sign it off rather than your client, as it emphasizes the issue of independence. In less sensitive circumstances it is a good idea to get the client to sign the letter, as it demonstrates their commitment to the exercise.

Questionnaire administration

Do not under-estimate the amount of work needed to process the questionnaires when they are returned. Of course, when dealing with numbers in excess of thirty you should use information technology to process the results. This will involve the answers from each ques- tionnaire being typed (or preferably scanned where very large numbers are involved) into a computer using a suitable software package that will ultimately process the data and produce meaningful information. There are software packages available to process questionnaires; however, many people use their favourite spreadsheet, database or statistical package. If you are not comfortable in dealing with this part of the process, make sure that you get the right people with the right skills to complete your data analysis. It is not an overly complex process, but it does need to be carried out in a systematic manner and requires lots of cross-checks built into the process to ensure the validity of the data.

Step 8: Reviewing your draft questionnaire with your client

Once you have reviewed your draft questionnaire with your client and agreed to the content and all the administrative arrangements surrounding the process, you then need to test it on a small number of between ten and twenty people to check that it is understandable. These people should be broadly representative of your final survey population. In selecting people for this process, try to select those who will be conscientious and so inclined to comment and add value to the final questionnaire design.

In conducting this review, ask the people involved to make a note of any difficult questions or confusing areas in the draft questionnaire. The feedback you will then receive will almost inevitably reveal flaws and problems with specific questions. The most common faults that are likely to emerge during this process are as follows:

- Using technical or organization jargon that is not understood by people
- Not using language or terminology that is familiar to people
- Including repetitive questions
- Asking inappropriate questions. For example,

you will lose credibility if you ask someone who does not supervise others a question on how he or she gets on with his or her staff

● Assuming that people have a complete understanding of the organization. For example, employees may not understand the phrase 'The operational board'.

Of course, not all the points raised may lead to changes, but you will almost invariably need to change some aspects of the questionnaire.

Step 9: Conducting the survey with your finalized questionnaire

Once all the points that have been raised in your pilot questionnaire have been noted and reviewed, your client should be given the opportunity to add, change or remove any questions. You are now ready to send out your final questionnaire together with an accompanying letter from your client.

You must make sure that all the administrative arrangements are in place and that the right people have been briefed about the exercise. The aim is to distribute your questionnaire and then to obtain as many completed replies as quickly as possible, and certainly within your project timescales, so that you can then begin your analysis phase.

On large-scale surveys involving many hundreds of people you may want to set up some telephone help lines to deal with any queries that people might have about the survey. But if you have planned everything and communicated clearly, there should be no major problems.

In presenting your survey feedback, you should use graphical outputs of the type that can easily be generated by today's software packages. Figure 4.6 provides a simple example.

The benefit of outputs like the one illustrated is that they immediately tell the story to clients and so are highly effective at communicating responses and indi-

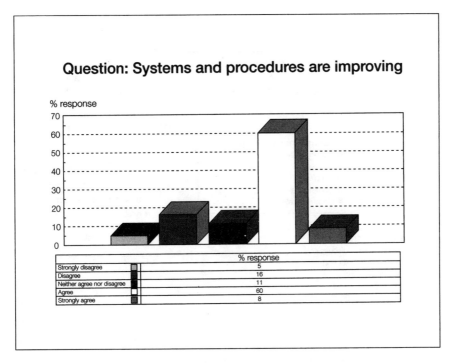

Figure 4.6   *Example of graphical questionnaire ouput*

cating trends. While you would need to back them up with a written report and detailed statistical data, the power of a graphical presentation is so much greater than that of the written word. Figure 4.7 provides a final overview of the questionnaire process.

PROCESS MAPPING

Process mapping has developed out of the recent surge in business process re-engineering techniques and their emphasis on identifying non-value added activities in organization processes. While not entirely new in origin, process mapping can be a very powerful way to build up a clear picture of how certain organizational processes work. To that extent, it is a very useful way of collecting and gathering information and is particularly relevant in re-organizations and information technology projects which require a detailed understanding of existing operations.

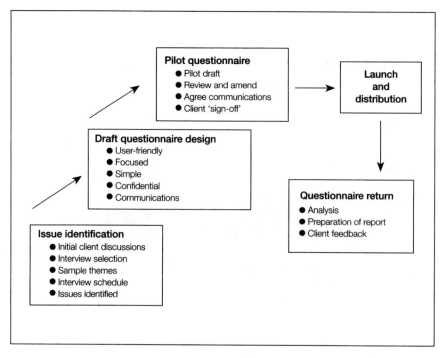

Figure 4.7   *Gathering information: the questionnaire process*

At the heart of the process mapping technique is the use of classic systems tools to produce flow diagrams. Figure 4.8 highlights some of the more readily used symbols and illustrates how they can be used to describe the various elements of a work process.

The aim in using these symbols is to build up a clear picture as to the precise steps or actions involved in a specific process, such as customer ordering or distribution.

Process mapping can be used to build up an understanding of almost any part of an organization. As an approach, it can render powerful insights into the amount of time a process takes and how much value added time is involved. Indeed, once you start using these symbols you will be surprised how easy it is to build up a detailed picture of a process. When applied in a re-engineering context, process mapping aims to assist in the identification and then removal of non-value added activities so as to produce more efficient

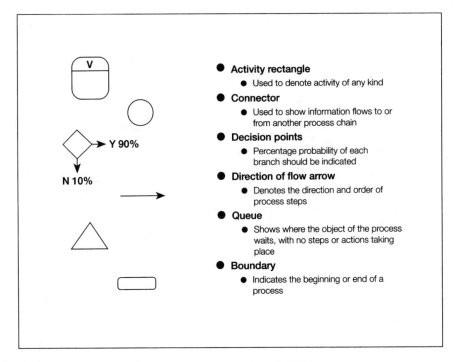

Figure 4.8 *Some classic process mapping definitions*

and leaner processes. Figure 4.9 details how value added activities can be identified using a simple decision tree. Of course, the notion of what actually constitutes a value added process in an organization can often be a controversial discussion. Nevertheless, the decision tree can help to pose the right questions for any review that you might be undertaking.

Process mapping involves five key stages and begins with a series of interviews:

- Interview job or process holders about what they actually do. This involves:
  - identifying critical or core processes
  - establishing the key steps and times to perform individual activities
  - identifying any wider organizational factors that might impact on the performance of the process
- Translate interview information into an initial process map

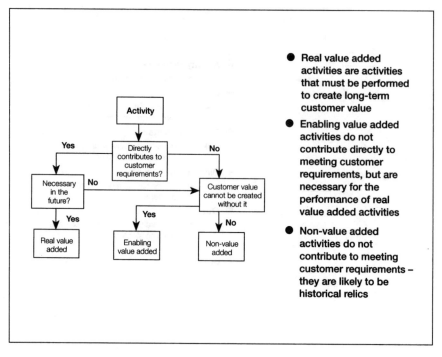

Figure 4.9 *How to classify value added and non-value added activities*

- Validate your process map with the process owner
  - check that you have understood everything
    - identify value added and non-value added time in the process
- Confirm the existing process map
  - discuss findings with your client
  - discuss findings with process holders
- Redesign the process to improve it or remove non-value added activities
  - involve client and process holders.

Process mapping can therefore be a very useful method of building up a clear picture of what is actually happening in parts of an organization. It is particularly useful in organization review projects that require a detailed understanding of existing processes. Figure 4.10 shows the way in which various activities are classified.

ACTIVITY DEFINITIONS

Class code	Definition	Classification
'V'	What the customer requires (Must do to produce product or service)	Value added
'Q'	Queue/wait state (Non moving, idle)	Non-value added
'I'	Inspection/Approval (Ensuring activity is performed correctly)	Non-value added
'M'	Transport, move (Moving from place to place)	Non-value added
'P'	Preparation (Preparing to work)	Non-value added
'R'	Redundant (Unnecessary activity)	Non-value added

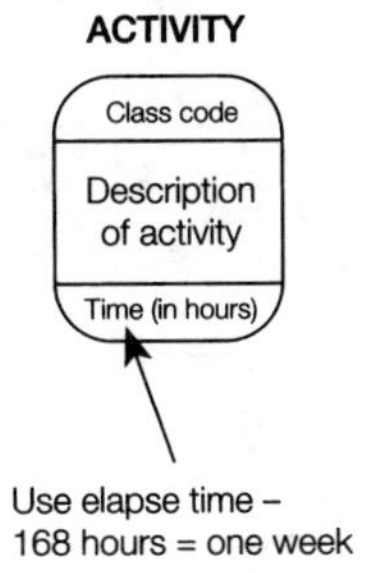

ACTIVITY

Class code

Description of activity

Time (in hours)

Use elapse time – 168 hours = one week

Figure 4.10 *What is driving performance?*

The whole approach can help you to build up a detailed understanding of processes, and Figure 4.11 illustrates a simple example involving a sales administration process. You can see how the various symbols are used to describe the key steps involved in this process and how significant this type of analysis can be in reviewing organizations.

In addition to developing process maps, another key element of the approach involves identifying wider organizational issues that might be impacting on the performance of a process. To obtain this type of information, you will need to use lots of the approaches we have identified in our section on interviewing.

While business process re-engineering has, in many organizations, achieved immense performance improvements, it has more recently become the subject of much criticism. Many organizations have applied the concept in an overly simplistic way, with the result that it has become associated with many crude and

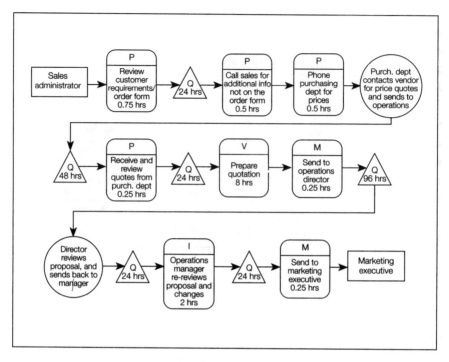

Figure 4.11 *Example of a process map*

brutal cost-cutting exercises. This may mean that some people immediately view process mapping techniques in a negative way. So when interviewing people you will need to be very sensitive to their concerns about the aims and objectives of your work. Nevertheless, the benefits that can result from process mapping can be considerable, so you should develop some ability in using the techniques. Listed below are two sets of questions that you can employ when interviewing job or process holders in trying to identify both the detailed aspects of their process and any organizational factors that might be impacting on the performance of the process.

Process analysis questions

- What are the inputs that start the process off?
- What are the functions or events that drive the process?
- Who are the suppliers (both internal and external) of the process?

- What are the outcomes or products of the process?
- Who are the ultimate customers of the process?
- What do you do next?
- Why do you then wait until x happens before completing that part of the process?
- Why do you record that information?
- What then happens to that information?
- Why do you have to refer that decision to x?
- Who uses the information you process?
- Can you describe the logical sequence of activities you perform to complete the process?
- How much time does each activity take to complete?
- How much queue (dead) time is there between activities?

Organizational issues questions

- How do your customers react to the responsiveness and quality of the outcomes of the process?
- What performance measures are in place to monitor the results of the process?
- What kinds of things prevent you from achieving better results in the process?
- Are there any other wider organizational issues that you feel need to be resolved to help the process to give better results?
- What factors annoy you about the way your department operates?
- If you had total freedom to improve the efficiency of your department, what specific things would you do?

UNDERSTANDING AND DEFINING YOUR CLIENT'S PROBLEM: BEING CLIENT FOCUSED

This stage of the consulting process involves the systematic collection of information in order to understand your client's underlying problem and begin developing possible solutions.

Questions you should ask

- How much detailed information do you need to collect?
- What information is already available within the organization?
- What other information will you need to collect?
- What research will you need to do?
- What methodologies will you need to use to collect information? (interviews, questionnaires, process mapping, observation, etc.)
- Whose involvement and support will you need?
- What kinds of costs will be involved, in terms of time, logistics and finance?
- How will you handle the issue of confidentiality during your information gathering work? What commitments/agreements will you give to your client(s)? What will you say to interviewees? What will you tell them about the next steps?
- How will you present your findings? What report presentation format will you use, and to what sort of client audience will you ultimately present?
- How are people around the organization going to react to the project and its aims?
- Are there any 'political' issues surrounding this project that you need to be aware of?

Client's perspective of you

- Do you give me the impression that you understand my problem?

- Do you agree with my analysis?
- Are you focusing on the right issues?
- Are you giving me confidence?
- Are you making me think differently about the problem?
- How long will this data collection process take, and how disruptive will it be to my operation and organization?
- Do you provide me with a sense of urgency?
- Are you throwing some new light on the problems?
- Are you listening to me and my concerns?

Other statements/questions you might use

- Can you tell me a little more about. . .?
- You mentioned earlier. . . . can you say more about that?
- Are you sure that x is a real problem?
- How do you know that x caused the problem?
- Can you explain. . .?
- Could you describe what actually happened. . .?
- Then what took place?
- Did anyone argue against it?
- But you said that this has been going on for many years and nothing has happened. Why has this been the case?
- How did that happen?
- Could you outline the strengths of the current situation?
- What are the weaknesses of the current situation?
- Are there any other potential risks?
- If you could do one thing to improve the situation, what would it be?

5 Action planning

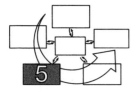

THE PLANNING PROCESS

The great danger with project management is that many people take the view that either they do not have the time to apply the disciplines or that they are simply unnecessary or over-complicated. These attitudes probably help to explain why so many projects fail or run away in terms of budget. As an internal consultant, at some time or other you will be asked to take on the role of a project manager, so you cannot afford to ignore the essential rules and techniques. In almost every project you become involved in you will need to apply some of the key practices of project management. As an internal consultant, you can always expect to be under pressure to deliver results and so you have to be able to not only manage your own time but also your client's time and resources. When you become involved in a very large project or have to run several small projects at the same time, you have to be able to project manage.

Of course, there will be some projects which are so complex that you will need to involve the services of a project management professional. This may be the case where you are involved in a major systems implementation which is using lots of people and equipment resources over a long period of time. In such cases you will probably use some form of project management software to deal with the detail that falls out of such projects. Many excellent project management software tools are now readily available to help you, and as part of your skills development you should become conversant with a package so that you can manage the essential elements.

Although there are a number of variations, the basic planning activities that are carried out by successful project managers can be divided into eight steps:

> 'Project sponsorship is critical. The importance of a project can often be measured by the level of its sponsor. Sponsorship also requires a personal commitment in terms of the sponsor's time, energy and focus. Sponsorship in name only may leave the internal consultant with a series of unresolved issues which may result in a project being overtaken by time or events, or simply faltering through lack of interest or progress. The bottom line is that you have to manage the project.'
>
> *Lewis Doyle*
> *Business Development Manager*
> *Legal and General*

- Assessing your project management skills
- Assessing how much planning you need to do
- Re-affirming your terms of reference
- Preparing a quick activity time chart
- Carrying out a risk analysis
- Preparing a detailed activity time chart for a high risk project
- Presenting your plan to your client
- Getting your client to sign off.

This planning process is presented in Figure 5.1.

Remember, you will have already prepared initial terms of reference and an initial plan when you were contracting with your client during your initial meetings phase. Action planning is simply an extension of these activities.

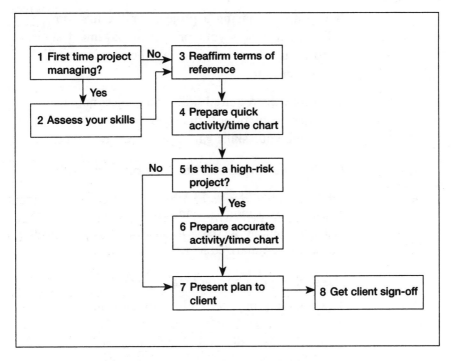

Figure 5.1   The planning process

Assessing your project management skills

As an internal consultant, you need a variety of skills in order to successfully plan, control and deliver the goals of a project. It has been said that a project manager needs to be the ultimate generalist, possessing a skill set made up of a great variety of talents.

One of the main reasons why projects fail is that the internal consultant lacks one or more of the key skills needed to manage a project or assignment successfully. For example, to monitor effectively the progress of a project against any plan, the work carried out must be formally recorded. This requires the skills of an administrator, who will carry out routine tasks and not get bored with detail. At the same time, you must also possess the skills of an analyst, negotiator, communicator, motivator and decision maker. When any one or more of these skills is missing, the danger is that a significant aspect of project management will either be ignored or overlooked. This invariably leads to poor control and a high probability of project failure.

If you are managing a project for the first time, you will need to assess your project management skills so as to ensure that you have all the required skills. So you will need to:

- review the required skills of a project manager
- assess your project manager skill set
- define your skills gap as a project manager.

Review the required skills of a project manager

There are a range of project management skills that any successful internal consultant needs to possess in order to manage successfully an assignment or project. These are summarized in Table 5.1.

Assessing your project manager skill set

The next step in determining any gaps in your project management skills is to assess your current skill set. Using the table of skills shown in Table 5.2, consider each skill area and estimate your effectiveness between

Table 5.1 Identifying the skills needed for managing client projects

Area	Activities	Skills needed
Planning	Define and agree terms of reference (the brief)	• Communicating with clients, management, experts and team • Listening and questioning • Analysing, summarizing and categorizing information • Effective writing • Negotiating • Motivating the consulting team
Planning	Task analysis to establish work breakdown	• Analysing the terms of reference into summarized headings
Planning	Establish task dependencies	• Analysing tasks for dependencies
Planning	Estimate task effort and task duration	• Communicating with clients • Analysing similar work
Planning	Determine project duration using a network chart	• Analysing to produce charts
Planning	Determine the critical path	• Analysing of plan
Planning	Allocate resources	• Communicating with your client to get resources • Negotiating • Analysing the plan
Risk analysis	Prepare initial risk analysis	• Analysing the plan • Communicating with clients
Risk analysis	Prepare contingency	• Analysing risk • Communicating with clients • Effective writing, report writing skills
Tracking and control	Track actual progress against plan	• Communicating with clients • Administrative work
Tracking and control	Regularly review progress against plan	• Communicating • Administrative work • Written work • Analysing the plan and actual work • Listening
Tracking and control	Replan if needed	• Decision making • Communicating with clients • Negotiating • Motivating • Analytical • Administrative work

1 and 10, with 1 indicating a poor capability and 10 indicating excellence. For example, as an administrator, if you believe you have good organizing skills and are adept at completing routine work, mark your skill level as 8.

Table 5.2 Assessing your personal skill set

Skill area	Skill level		
	Poor		Excellent
Administrator – Organizing – Routine work	1-----2-----3-----4-----5-----6-----7-----8-----9-----10		
Analyst – Problem solving – Mathematics	1-----2-----3-----4-----5-----6-----7-----8-----9-----10		
Negotiator – Innovative and informed – Patient	1-----2-----3-----4-----5-----6-----7-----8-----9-----10		
Verbal communication – Clear speech – Logical thoughts	1-----2-----3-----4-----5-----6-----7-----8-----9-----10		
Written communication – Expressing ideas on paper – Presenting information	1-----2-----3-----4-----5-----6-----7-----8-----9-----10		
Listening – Attentive – Patient	1-----2-----3-----4-----5-----6-----7-----8-----9-----10		
Motivating – Leadership qualities – Commanding respect	1-----2-----3-----4-----5-----6-----7-----8-----9-----10		
Decision making – Listening and deciding – Courage and conviction	1-----2-----3-----4-----5-----6-----7-----8-----9-----10		

Determining your skills gap as a project manager

Once you have assessed your skill set score, record your results in the first row in Table 5.3. Highlight any column where your score is 7 or less.

Table 5.3 Identifying your skills gap as a project manager

Activities	ADM	ANA	NEG	VER	WRI	LIS	MOT	DEC
Your score								
Defining and agreeing terms of reference (the consulting brief)	✓	✓	✓	✓	✓	✓	✓	
Task analysis to establish work breakdown		✓						
Establishing task dependencies		✓						
Estimating task effort and task duration		✓		✓				
Determining the project's duration using a network chart		✓						
Determining the critical path		✓						
Allocating resources		✓	✓	✓				
Preparing an initial risk analysis		✓		✓				
Preparing contingency plans		✓		✓	✓			
Tracking actual progress against plan	✓			✓				
Regularly reviewing progress against plan	✓	✓		✓	✓	✓		
Replanning if needed	✓	✓	✓	✓			✓	✓

If any highlighted row has a tick in it, then you need to take action. You will need to either increase your skill level in that area, for example, through additional training, or possibly consider using other, more skilled people in your team to carry out the activities. Remember, effective project management demands that all these activities be carried out to a high standard.

Assessing how much planning you need to do

After you have identified the effectiveness of your skill set to manage projects and made provisions to overcome any weaknesses, your next step is to determine how much detail is needed in any plan. Figure 5.2 highlights the options open to you in assessing the complexity/risk dimension, but the general rule is that if a project is high-risk then you have to plan in more detail. Review our section on 'Carrying out risk

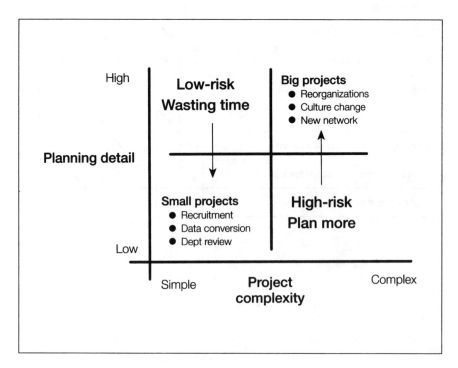

Figure 5.2   How much planning?

analysis' in this chapter to determine the level of risk you may have on a particular project.

Complex projects are typically large ones, such as corporate re-organizations, cultural changes and installations of large computer networks. These are usually high-risk projects, and they do require more detailed planning. Smaller and less complex projects may involve, for example, a small training needs analysis, a data conversion project or the review of a small department. The complexity of a project can be defined as one where there are many tasks, many task dependencies and many resources. It is also likely that complex projects will take several months to complete.

Your next planning step in managing a project is to re-affirm your terms of reference and then, irrespective of the complexity of the project, develop a quick activity time chart. If you have determined that the level of risk for a project is high, you will have to prepare a more detailed activity time chart.

Reaffirming your terms of reference

'Get a clear set of goals, responsibilities and processes in your terms of reference.'

Peter Brunner, Internal Consultant Company Development and Communications,
Mercedes-Benz AG

Your terms of reference must be regularly referred to throughout the course of any project. They should also be updated as and when necessary. Occasionally, the objectives may change during the life of a project. These changes must be documented in your terms of reference, but it is equally essential that any changes are discussed in detail and agreed by your client before they are implemented. You do not have the power to change your terms of reference without the express agreement of your client.

At this stage you need to re-examine your initial terms of reference and amend any of the sections that you previously included. These sections are:

- Background
- Objectives
- Boundary
- Constraints
- Assumptions
- Client reporting
- Project deliverables
- Activity time chart
- Finance.

> 'Be clear on the expected outcomes of the project; know what the objectives and scope of the work are. If initially they appear vague then get your client's direct agreement or permission to shape a clearer remit for the task.'
>
> *Lewis Doyle*
> *Business Development Manager*
> *Legal and General*

Most of your effort in re-affirming your terms of reference will be directed towards preparing a quick activity time chart (see next section) which shows all the additional tasks that you have identified at this stage of your planning, together with an estimate of the resource effort and duration, plus a more accurate estimate of the costs. If you plan in detail, you will obtain the estimated project end date and the start and finish dates for each task. You will also know when to make your key deliverables, such as the delivery of a report or start-up of a system. In some cases you will be given the end date for a project and you will need to work backwards to determine whether the start date for the project is feasible. Your activity time chart will be the focus for most of these activities, so it takes on a very important role in your project management activities.

INSIGHT

Avoid losing sight of your terms of reference as your project progresses. This is a classic error on the part of an internal consultant. Constant referral to your terms of reference will ensure that you keep on track with your work and avoid surprising your client.

Preparing a quick activity time chart

'Be thorough and set standards for your own work and behaviour that exceed your clients' expectations.'

Dalim Basu, Project Manager, Independent Television Network

At this stage in projects there are too many unknown factors, such as additional objectives or requirements that still have to be identified, or too many assumptions still to be resolved. This can prevent most project managers from preparing a classic activity time chart, or Gantt Chart, that requires detailed information, in which case you should just prepare a simple one using the information you already have. This should be easy to prepare, but you must be ready to accept less accuracy as to when your project will end. You may also not have any clear indication of the critical tasks – namely, the ones that you cannot afford to delay. Inevitably there are consequences of adopting a less detailed approach, but for many low risk projects which are not going to last long, a quick activity time chart will be sufficient for you to control the various activities.

Your starting point is to use your activity time chart in your initial terms of reference and add more detail by carrying out the following steps:

- Identify detailed tasks
- Establish task dependencies
- Allocate resources
- Estimate effort and duration for each task
- Calculate costs.

Identify detailed tasks

Your initial terms of reference may only contain four or five activities to describe what has to be done on the project and when. For each activity, note down all those tasks that need to be carried out in order to complete the activity. This approach of translating your initial terms of reference into activities and then tasks is called the Work Breakdown Structure (WBS). For larger projects it may be more convenient to introduce a higher level called a stage, so the order would be stage, activity and then task.

Examine the WBS in the example of a detailed activity time chart for a project involving a training needs analysis shown in Figure 5.3. Note that there are tasks which have no people or effort allocated to them. These are known as milestones and, as the name suggests, they are key events which occur during the life of a project. Milestones therefore act as a focus, showing the targets that the project is aiming to hit and the times when things need to be delivered.

Establish task dependencies

This stage of planning identifies the relationship between each task on your detailed activity time chart. In most cases, when you build up your chart, you will normally place the tasks in the order that they need to be done. Noting down the preceding task in the 'Prev' column makes it easier to identify which task must end before the next one can start. This can be seen in the example activity time chart by referring to task 4.1, 'Develop individual action plan'. It is not clear by just looking at the chart which task must end before this one can start. However, if you refer to the column headed 'Prev' you will note that it depends on both tasks 2.7 and 3.4 ending. In addition, if you later decide to prepare a more accurate detailed activity time chart, having identified the predecessor tasks will make this process easier to complete.

Allocate resources

Now you need to identify and allocate the available resources to each task on your detailed activity time chart. Under the heading 'Who', note the initials of the people who will work on that task. If more than one person will work on a single task, place them on a new line. This makes it easier to identify and add up their effort in order to calculate the total chargeable

Action	Who	Effort	Prev	Start	Wk1	Wk2	Wk3	Wk4	Wk5	Wk6	Wk7	Wk8
Activity 1 - Requirements												
1. Form steering group	NG	0.5			**							
	CW	0.5			**							
2. Agree target department	C	0.5	1.1		**							
3. Analyse department	CW	2	1.2		***							
4. Determine competencies	CW	2	1.3			***						
5. Agree competency map	C	0.5	1.4			**						
	CW	0.5	1.4			**						
6. Deliver requirements document	CW	0	1.5			*						
Activity 2 - Analysis												
1. Design questionnaire	CW	1	1.6			**	*					
2. Agree questionnaire	NG	0.5	2.1				**					
	CW	0.5	2.1				**					
3. Send out questionnaire	CW	0.5	2.2					**				
4. Analyse returned questionnaires	CW	2	2.3						***			
5. Document findings	CW	1	2.4						**			
6. Discuss results	CW	0.5	2.5							**		
	NG	0.5	2.5							**		
	C	0.5	2.5							**		
7. Deliver results document	CW	0	2.6							*		
Activity 3 - Methods												
1. Identify methods	CW	1	1.6				**	*				
2. Review systems	CW	2	3.1					***				
3. Document findings	CW	1	3.2					**				
4. Deliver methods document	CW	0	3.3					*				
Activity 4 - Recommendations												
1. Develop individual action plan	CW	3	2,7,3,4							****	*	
2. Prepare report	CW	2	4.1								***	
3. Present results	NG	0.5	4.2									*
	CW	0.5	4.2									*
	C	0.5	4.2									*
4. Deliver recommendations	CW	0	4.3									*
Activity 5 - Management												
1. Project management @ 0.5d/w	CW	3.5	1.1		*****	*****	*****	*****	*****	*****	*****	
2. Review meetings @ 0.5d/w	NG	3.5	1.1		*****	*****	*****	*****	*****	*****	*****	
	CW	3.5	1.1		*****	*****	*****	*****	*****	*****	*****	

Estimated Costs

Resource Name:	CW–Chris Worthing	**Rate:** $800	**Effort:** 27	**Cost:** $21,600
Resource Name:	NG–Norma Good	**Rate:** $1,200	**Effort:** 5.5	**Cost:** $6,600
Resource Name:	C–Committee	**Rate:** $3,600	**Effort:** 2	**Cost:** $7,200
Resource Name:		**Rate:**	**Effort:**	**Cost:**
Equipment Name:	Hire audio-visual equipment			**Cost:** $1,200
Equipment Name:				**Cost:**
Expenses:	Travel and accommodation			**Cost:** $3,000

Total Estimated Costs: $39,600

Figure 5.3 Detailed plan activity time chart

time they will spend on the project. This will also facilitate the preparation of their schedule after you have estimated their effort and duration (see next section) for each task. At the bottom of the chart in the section 'Estimated costs', note down the individual's initials and name.

If you have a choice of people when allocating to tasks, you must consider factors such as the project's status, people's experience, their past performance, other work commitments as well as time off for holiday and training needs. The time taken to complete each task will vary depending on the resource you have chosen, or been given. This in turn may have an effect on the end date for the project. Developing a good network of contacts within your organization will help you get background information on the people you are working with and help you in making the right resourcing decisions.

Estimate effort and duration for each task

When planning projects, you must be clear about the distinction between effort and duration for a task. For most people this is a confusing issue, and you can expect to be called upon to explain the difference by people who are not conversant with project management.

Effort is the time taken by someone to do the actual work. Duration, also referred to as elapsed time, is the time taken to complete a task and includes all the non-productive time, such as non-working hours, holidays and time off for sickness. The relationship between the two can be expressed as follows:

$$\text{Duration} = \text{Effort} + \text{Non-productive time}$$

For example, writing a report might require two hours' effort. However, if you begin writing this report at 8 am, stopping for a meeting at 9 am followed by other activity during the day, and then resuming at 5 pm for the last hour, then the effort would be two hours, but the duration is one day (ten hours). Why do you need to know the difference? Well, effort is used to schedule people's working time and is also used to calculate time that may ultimately be charged to your client depending on the financial arrangements surrounding your work. Duration is used to identify when an individual task ends.

When preparing either a quick or detailed activity time chart, for each person working on a task start by estimating the effort required to do that task and then work out the duration. You do this by estimating how long each person would take to do the task if he or she did nothing else but work continuously on that task. You then estimate all the non-productive time.

For example, the effort required by a project manager to form a steering committee might be half a day, but the duration may be over a two-day period, as he or she would be waiting for other people to return telephone calls to confirm the scheduling of the committee's time and the booking of a meeting room. During the same two-day period, your client may also spend half a day informally briefing the proposed committee on the nature of the project before they are appointed to the role. So the total effort would be two half-days (i.e. one day effort) and the duration would be two days.

For each task on your activity time chart, estimate the effort required by each person to complete the task and note this down as a figure in the 'Day effort' column. Next note down the duration under the appropriate week headings 'Wk 1', 'Wk 2' etc. Don't forget to take into account staff time requirements for holidays, sickness, training and commitments to other work. As a general rule, the duration of a task can take up to four times as long as the effort required to complete that task.

You can now enter the start date for the project under the heading 'Start' and continue down the column entering the start date for each task. If you are given an end date for your project, enter this against the last task and work up the column entering the start date for each task. You now have an activity time chart which shows the overall duration of your project with specific start dates for each task.

INSIGHT

Increasing the effort on a task does not always decrease its duration. For example:
- **When writing computer code, increasing the number of developers will decrease the duration. But if there are more developers than computers available, increasing the number of developers will not affect the duration of the task, but it will increase the costs.**
- **Planning a trip. Increasing the number of transport crew will not decrease the duration of the trip.**
- **A meeting. Increasing the number of participants at a meeting usually increases the duration.**

Calculate costs

'Finance drives projects. Never overlook detail. This will filter out the winners from the losers.'

Alan Goodson, Research and Development, Dow Chemicals

Managing costs is a fundamental part of the project management process and estimating the cost for a project is a task which you, as a project manager, must complete and feedback to your client. Most organizations will make a distinction between 'real money' and 'internal money'. The importance of estimating the value of real money is self-evident. This is money that your organization will be spending on external services and needs to be tightly controlled. Estimating and reporting the value of internal money will depend on whether your organization 'charges' for its services internally within the organization.

To determine the costs for your project, enter the monetary rate for each person at the bottom of the activity time chart and note down the addition of the total effort for each resource under the 'Who' column. Multiply the rate by the effort and you will determine the cost for that person. At the bottom of the chart you will be able to enter one-off charges, such as for the hire of equipment, and a line to enter any expenses that may occur. Now you can add up all the costs and obtain the total estimated costs for the project.

Carrying out a risk analysis

This step is often omitted from a detailed plan as it is often thought too difficult or time-consuming to prepare. This is a misconception, as the process for preparing a risk analysis involves only the following two steps:

- Identifying high-risk tasks
- Preparing contingency tasks.

Identifying high-risk tasks

This planning step is a structured process for anticipating those tasks that will potentially lead to a crisis during your project. Once you have identified these high-risk tasks, you will need to prepare a contingency plan to deal with them.

To carry out a risk analysis for each task on your plan, you need to:

- Determine the probability of failure of that task using a high, medium or low scale
- Determine the impact on project if it does fail to happen on a high, medium or low scale.

An example of a risk analysis on a project that required a team of key people to go to an airport to catch an important and restricted aeroplane flight would be as shown in Figure 5.4.

Preparing contingency tasks

After you have recorded your risk assessment, you will need to highlight the tasks that have a medium or high ranking for both the 'Probability of Failure' and 'Impact on the Project'. These are your high-risk tasks, and a contingency plan of action needs to be made for each one. You will then need to record the contingency actions as tasks in your plan.

TASK	PROBABILITY OF FAILURE	IMPACT ON PROJECT
Oversleep	Low	High
Work callout	High	Medium
Car breakdown	Low	High
Accident	Low	High
Traffic problems	High	Medium
Airport strike	Low	High

High-risk tasks

Figure 5.4 *Identifying high-risk tasks during risk analysis*

Preparing a detailed activity time chart for a high-risk project

If you have determined that your project is high-risk, there are two further techniques involving your activity time chart which can give you additional and more accurate information to manage the project. These techniques involve:

- determining the project duration using a network chart
- determining the critical path.

When preparing an activity time chart which forms the major part of your plan, you must balance accuracy against speed. The decision to adopt either approach will be determined by the nature of your project. Typically, producing a quick plan will be sufficient for short projects lasting a few weeks. A quick plan may also be suitable for more complex longer projects if the objectives are still being debated and there is an urgency to start 'doing things'. As a general rule, make your decision after you have carried out a simple risk assessment on your project (see section on carrying out a risk analysis). For high-risk projects, you must prepare an accurate activity time chart.

Determining a project's duration by using a network chart

The overall duration of your client's project is calculated by producing and analysing a network chart. A network chart can be summarized as something which:

- is a schematic representation of all the tasks that make up your project or assignment
- shows the order and sequence in which the work must be completed
- shows the dependencies of each task involved in the project
- is a route map of all the tasks in an assignment – a map showing all the stations of an underground railway is much easier to understand than a written description for the location of all stations.

To build up a network chart, you only need to know the tasks, the preceding tasks and the duration. Once that is completed, you can analyse the network chart to:

- calculate the total duration of your project
- determine the critical path.

To calculate the total duration of an assignment or project, you need to calculate for each task what are termed the Early Start and the Late Start. These are defined as:

- Early Start (ES) This is the earliest time that a task can start on your project. Start from the first task and use the following formula to calculate the succeeding task's ES:

ES for succeeding = ES from preceding + Duration of preceding

If there is more than one preceding task, calculate all possible ESs and take the highest value.

- Late Start (LS) This is the latest time that a task can start. Work backwards through the network from the final task and use the following formula to calculate the preceding task's LS:

LS for preceding = LS from succeeding − Duration of preceding

If there is more than one succeeding task, calculate all possible LSs and take the lowest value.

There are two other terms that you need to be familiar with. These are Slack and Assignment Duration, and are defined as follows:

- Slack is the difference between LS and ES. If this is greater than 0 (i.e. you have slack time in deciding when to begin this task), then you can take more time over the task if you begin at the ES. You allocate your less experienced people to the task, as you have slack time in case of slippage
- Assignment Duration is calculated from the last task. This is the addition of the ES and the duration of the last task.

The techniques for actually building the network chart involve the following.

Using symbols to build a network chart

Typically, you develop a network chart by using boxes divided into four sections to represent tasks as shown below:

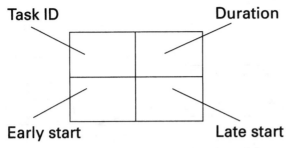

Task ID   Duration

Early start   Late start

Use arrows to show the dependencies of the tasks.

Give each task a unique number in ascending order and place this in the top left corner.

An arrow between two tasks means that the second task cannot start until the first one has been completed:

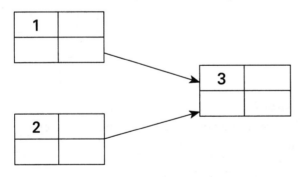

In the following example, tasks 1 and 2 must both finish before task 3 can begin:

In the following example, tasks 1 and 2 must both finish before task 3 begins and tasks 4 and 5 cannot begin until task 3 has been completed.

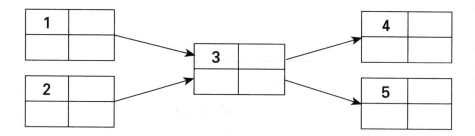

Note that the flow of tasks is from left to right.

Network patterns to avoid

When building up a network chart, try to avoid the following patterns:

Redundant links

The link between task 1 and task 4 is redundant because task 4 is dependent on task 3 which is dependent on task 2 which in turn is dependent on task 1.

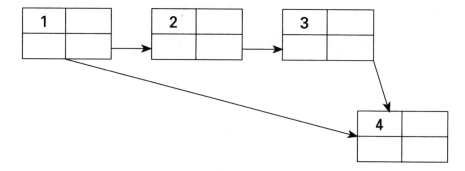

Looping tasks

None of these tasks can begin or end because they are all dependent on each other.

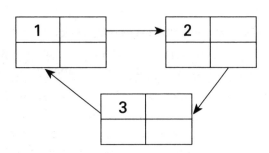

Hanging tasks

Nothing happens after task 4 is complete. Avoid this unless task 4 is the last task.

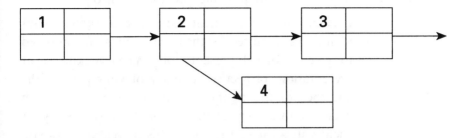

Determining the critical path

From your network chart you produce your critical path, which is the longest route of tasks through the project. The benefit of determining the critical path is that you will know which tasks cannot be delayed without impacting on the end date of your whole project.

The critical path is also the chain of tasks where the Early start and Late start are the same, that is, when there is no slack. In effect, you have no choice as to when these tasks must start.

Presenting your plan to your client

After your plan is completed, you must present it to your client. Send a copy of the plan to them a few days ahead of your agreed meeting. This will give them time to review the details and prepare any questions they may have.

Getting client sign-off

It is critical that your client fully agrees with your detailed plan, and it is only when they sign off the plan that your implementation work can really begin. In some cases it may not be practical for your client to physically sign your detailed plan document as they may be working elsewhere in the organization, but you must receive written confirmation from them that you can proceed according to the presented plan. This important step will avoid any misunderstanding at a later stage as the objectives, boundary and reporting requirements are presented in your detailed plan.

In some cases your client may have to present your plan to a committee for their approval, so be prepared to give a formal presentation. When making your presentation, project a summary of your plan to the audience, discussing the main points, and provide each person with a copy of the details. In most cases your client will want you to make this presentation as you will have all the detailed knowledge to answer questions from the committee.

The next stage in the internal consulting process is implementation, and this is where the real work begins on the project, with the appropriate parts of the plan communicated to all the project team members. The project is then tracked and controlled by the project manager and regular feedback is presented to your client. These actions are discussed in more detail in the next chapter.

ACTION PLANNING: BEING CLIENT FOCUSED

This stage involves formulating your detailed plans in preparation for any implementation stage. This stage of the consulting cycle will involve you carrying out many detailed project management activities.

Questions you should ask

▶ Are you confident about your project management skills and capability?

▶ Will the resources that will be required to implement your proposed recommendations – people, management commitment, finance and other resources generate a favourable or negative response from your client?

▶ Are the timescales you are suggesting realistic?

- Are there available processes in place to project manage the implementation phase?
- Are your recommendations appropriate? Check and audit them for complexity, feasibility, practicality, etc.
- Have all responsibilities for the implementation process been defined?
- Have you identified the critical path and developed any necessary contingency plans?
- Is your client fully committed to moving forward?

Client's perspective of you

- Are your implementation plans practical and feasible?
- Have you adequately considered the costs and potential disruption involved?
- Have you adequately advised me of the project planning processes?
- Have you considered the timing and the other implications.

Other client thoughts

- Do I want to continue?
- Is this going to work?
- Are we still on track?
- Is your advice sound?
- I will need to think about this and discuss it with my colleagues.
- So how does that relate to your earlier observations?
- That's a difficult one to resolve.
- So how might we deal with that issue?
- We may need to spend more time on this.

Other statements/questions you might use

- So we would like to discuss the options for moving ahead.

- It is our view that it will be difficult to progress without addressing the resourcing issues on. . . .

- We realize that there may be some difficult decisions involved here.

- We did think you would need time to reflect on the options and consequences.

- We feel we have been realistic about the resourcing and timing.

- We would be happy to work with x to develop the details and implementation timetable.

- We believe you will need to question, solicit, challenge and marshal the x of y. . . .

- We are not sure that would work because of. . . .

- We recognize that you will need to take some of your colleagues through the analysis.

6 Implementation

THE IMPLEMENTATION PROCESS

'The normal state of a project is chaotic and hectic. A project that is going well is just about to go wrong.'

Tony Edgar, Senior Manager, Lloyds Bank

Implementation is the stage in our consulting process where the real work on a project begins. The key stages involved are summarized in Figure 6.1. Your main role at this stage is to make things happen using your terms of reference and activity time chart which form your overall implementation plan.

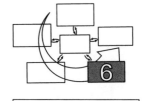

As we have said, the nature of your involvement in any implementation phase will depend on the project

'Draw in other skills and like-minded people as appropriate. This again comes back to the status of your sponsor. Get the right sponsor and obtaining the right calibre of people and resources will not cause you undue problems.'

Lewis Doyle
Business Development Manager
Legal and General

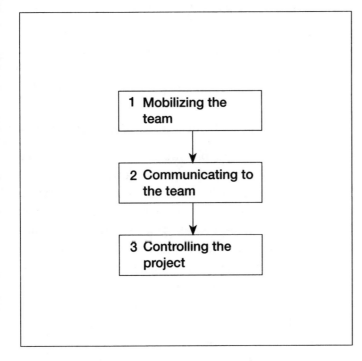

Figure 6.1 The implementation process

and your client's perspective. But in many cases you will be expected to drive through an implementation plan in conjunction with your client and their team.

INSIGHT

Remember, things don't happen by themselves, you have to make them happen. Use your terms of reference and activity time chart to execute the project. You have to take the initiative and drive through the necessary tasks to completion.

The implementation process is made up of three steps:

- Mobilizing the team
- Communicating to the team
- Controlling the project.

MOBILIZING THE TEAM

After your plan has been signed off by the client, you have to mobilize all the team members involved in the project. This involves contacting all the team members to:

- advise them that they will be working on the project
- ensure that they are ready to participate in the project
- begin motivating them towards the objectives.

In some cases, the people you thought were available to implement the project might no longer be available and others may have to be substituted in their place. So expect to have to manage resourcing problems. Sometimes resources, including both people and equipment, will not be available and you will have to begin immediately to assess the impact of this on your project. In such cases, finding alternative resources, changing your plan and communicating all this back to your client becomes a priority issue and is part of everyday project management.

On some projects, your involvement during the implementation phase will be to assist a full-time project manager. Your knowledge and input in such situations is very important, as only you and your client will have a detailed understanding of the project. You may also have discussed the project earlier with a number of people to assess their involvement in the implementation. So re-establishing contact with them during your mobilization stage and introducing them to the project manager will be much easier.

COMMUNICATING TO THE TEAM

Once you have contacted all the people involved in the project and confirmed their availability, you then need to send a confirmation document to each of them. This details their individual responsibilities and explains how their contribution fits into the overall project plan. You will need to follow up this written document with a meeting to discuss any other specific issues that may arise. In most cases you will want to have a large project team meeting to discuss the working arrangements in detail.

To summarize your activity at this stage, you need to:

- send a document to each person outlining their responsibilities
- follow this up with a meeting to clarify issues.

Your document and subsequent presentation to each member of the implementation team should contain the following information:

- A condensed version of the terms of reference
- A summary of the activity time chart
- All the detail from the activity time chart, including task names, individual responsibilities and start and end dates
- A covering letter from your client, welcoming everyone to the team. Of course, it is better if your client is also able to attend the meeting and outline their aspirations concerning the project.

CONTROLLING THE PROJECT

> 'Don't take a purist approach to implementation and expect to attain 100 per cent acceptance of your proposals or believe that they will never be subject to amendment. Stay realistic about what can be attained and in what timescales.'
>
> *Lewis Doyle*
> *Business Development Manager*
> *Legal and General*

In almost every project, things change. It is very rare that a project follows the plan as exactly represented in your activity time chart. Controlling a project involves being clear as to where you are. It also involves replanning where necessary to meet the objectives in your terms of reference. This control process is shown in Figure 6.2 and is summarized by the following steps:

- Tracking the implementation team's progress against the plan
- Reviewing the plan
- Replanning to meet the project objectives.

Tracking the team's progress against the plan

'Communicate your plans, deliverables, target dates and progress as relevant, and publicise your achievements.'

Dalim Basu, Project Manager, Independent Television Network

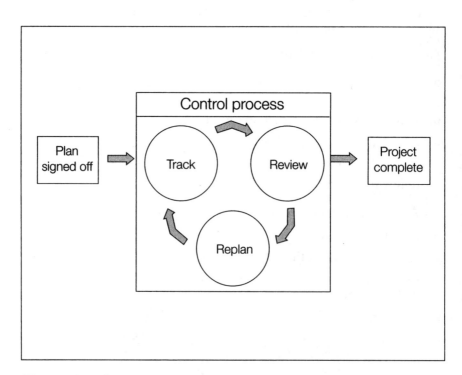

Figure 6.2 *The control process*

As the project manager, you need to communicate regularly to each team member to find out what tasks he or she has completed and, more importantly, what tasks and parts of a task have yet to be completed. It is always crucial to determine how much more time is required to complete a task.

For example, if the scope for a task called 'interview team' was changed so that the team size increased from five to ten people, then, although you may already have completed two days of interviewing, you now still have eight days left. Your original plan would show that two days were completed and three days were left. Being aware of this situation will allow you to replan and feed back accurate information to your client.

Contacting each team member to determine this information will take up a considerable amount of your time, but the information you gather will keep your project on course. The easiest way to gather this information is to ensure that everyone completes a weekly time sheet of the tasks they have to carry out. You can then update your activity time chart to show this information.

Using timesheets is a valuable tool in gathering information, but you also need to follow this up with a quick meeting or telephone call to discuss how much more time will be required to complete all remaining tasks and to feed back information to the person on how the whole project is progressing. Everyone on an implementation team likes to know what is going on as well as the client.

Reviewing the plan

'The internal consultant must keep abreast of developments.'
Peter Stewart, Business Development Manager, PowerGen UK

During any project you will be holding regular meetings with various people, including the project team members, client(s) and, in some cases, steering committees. The focus for each discussion will differ depending on which person or group you meet. Higher-level discussions confirming the objectives and monitoring progress at key stages of a project will often take place with a steering committee that has been established to oversee the work. More detailed work, focusing on activity levels, would be discussed at individual client meetings, while individual task details would be covered with the team member responsible for completing that task.

Holding regular reviews with all these parties allows you to:

- confirm all the estimates for outstanding work
- agree all new tasks and other changes
- confirm the continued validity of your terms of reference.

The responsibility for holding these meetings will rest with different people depending on the level in the project. Table 6.1 summarizes the frequency of these review meetings, highlighting who is responsible for organizing them. For example, a person on a steering committee would be responsible for organizing the next meeting, where you will present the latest information at a stage level. Normally these meetings

Table 6.1

LEVEL	RESPONSIBILITY	FREQUENCY
Stage	Steering committee	Monthly
Activity	Client	Bi-weekly
Activity	Project manager	Weekly
Task	Team member	Weekly

will occur on a monthly basis. You should expect to hold a client meeting at least every two weeks to discuss progress at an activity level. Individual project team members will be responsible for sending you their weekly reports or timesheets and discussing issues at your weekly or daily meetings.

INSIGHT

Even though it may be another person's responsibility to arrange a progress meeting, take the initiative and offer a tactful reminder. This will increase the possibility of the meeting taking place.

Replanning to meet the project objectives

After holding a regular review meeting, you may have identified that you have slipped on your plan and that you need to take corrective action. Before you change your activity time chart, there are a number of actions that you must consider. These are discussed below.

Offer incentives

Consider offering incentives for completing tasks on time. Of course, you may well be restricted by your budget in doing this, so you must check with your client first. In such cases, offering overtime or bonus payments can be beneficial if the project is critical and important enough.

Increase resources

If your budget allows, consider adding more people to your project team, using temporary staff or purchasing more equipment to complete tasks. But again, check with your client first to get budget approval.

Negotiate with your client

If unforeseen circumstances have arisen, you may well need to negotiate with your client to get an extension to the completion date for the project. You should only ever use this tactic in extreme situations, as you will lose credibility if you do this more than once. It is very much a matter of last resort.

Negotiate with suppliers

If your project implementation has been disrupted by a supplier, try to reach an agreement with them whereby partial deliveries are made or some other compromise arrangement so as to prevent the project from failing.

Review your work schedule

Identify those tasks that can be delayed without impacting on the end date of your project. Then reschedule the starting date of each of those tasks. This will release people from those tasks so that they can be allocated to the other more important and critical tasks in order to keep your project on track.

IMPLEMENTATION: BEING CLIENT FOCUSED

This stage of the consulting cycle involves you managing the detailed project implementation.

Questions you should ask

- Have you secured your client's agreement to the plan?
- Are you confident about your project management skills and capability?
- Have you prepared a briefing pack for the implementation team?
- Have you spoken to each individual team member?
- Will there be any conflicts arising with other parts of the organization as your work develops?
- Have you spent sufficient time thinking about the balance and composition of your team?
- Have you communicated with relevant suppliers and other interested parties?

- Do you have the necessary control and reporting procedures in place?
- Have you agreed regular access to your client during the implementation period?

Client's perspective of you

- Are you competent?
- Does everything seem to be under control?
- Am I getting regular updates of progress?
- Have I been involved in the important meetings?
- Does it all seem realistic and feasible?
- Are you capable of taking people along with the changes?

Other statements/questions you might use

- We would welcome your attendance at the launch meeting.
- Perhaps you would be prepared to welcome people and outline your expectations.
- We are experiencing some problems with Department X and would like to discuss it with you before it becomes a big issue.
- Here are the key developments arising out of last week's work.
- We are still on track.
- How do you think things are progressing?
- What feedback have you received from other people concerning progress?
- We may have to re-allocate some people/resources for that stage of the plan, but we do not foresee any slippage on the overall plan.
- We may need to re-negotiate some extra time or resources as a result of last week's problems.

7 Reviewing and exiting projects

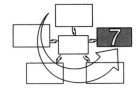

WHY SIGN OFF A PROJECT?

A critical action at the end of any assignment is to ensure that your project's completion is formally agreed and 'signed off' by your client. It is important to let your client know that your involvement has formally ended and that any additional work will need to be subject to a new agreement.

As a successful internal consultant, your time will be at a premium, with many clients requesting your attention and service, so you must manage their expectations. If, as a result of poor client management, you lead your clients to believe that they have endless freedom to call upon your time you will never be able to operate successfully. Of course, clients can contact you at any time and, indeed, that is something that you should actively promote. However, there is a difference between being able to contact you and then wanting an immediate and total response. Your clients, just like you, will need to recognize that you have other clients and commitments and that it is not possible for you to meet all their demands at the same time. So educating your clients with regard to these commitments without upsetting them is a key challenge – particularly when the client thinks justifiably that their problem should take precedence over all others. But you have to do this, and exiting and formally 'signing off' from projects is part of this educative process. You must also conclude your assignment in a positive and friendly manner which preserves your client relationship and ensures that they will call you for another project.

Exiting an assignment is achieved by using your original terms of reference and presenting your client with a report that will include:

- a review of various aspects of the project
- a review of your own performance.

Figure 7.1 presents an overview of this process. Of course, the complexity of the assignment will determine the amount of detail you need to present in your review report.

The benefits of using this process to sign off a project are:

- having a structured method for conducting your review
- getting feedback on your contribution and performance
- measuring the effectiveness of your work and the success of the project's results.

This review will also help you to maintain your professional relationship with your client and prevent you from being branded an 'in and out' type of consultant.

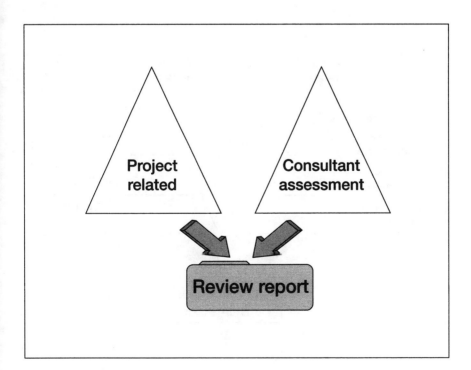

Figure 7.1   *The review process*

Maintaining a positive and friendly relationship at the end of a project preserves a positive client image. A review also signals a strong commitment to your client that will help to place you first on their list when next commissioning consultancy assistance.

THE REVIEW PROCESS

The two parts of your review process, dealing with your own assessment and the project assessment, can be divided into a number of specific activities. These are presented in Figure 7.2 which shows that more effort must be directed towards the activities at the bottom of each triangle. As a minimum, you should carry out the top two activities from each assessment, which are:

● a self-assessment

● assessment of you by your client

● the effectiveness of the project

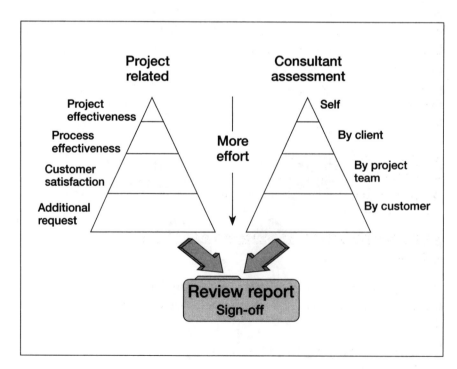

Figure 7.2 *The review process*

- the effectiveness of the planning and implementation process.

The other activities should be carried out if you have the required resources and funds to complete them. These include:

- assessment of you by the project team
- assessment of you by the customer
- determining customer satisfaction of the project
- gathering requests and recommendations for further improvements and changes.

For each of these activities, you need to gather information from relevant people. So, apart from your own self-assessment, each of these activities will normally take the form of a series of one-to-one interviews between yourself and other parties. You need to structure your interviews so that you ask a series of standard questions prepared in advance. Of course, you also need to allow an interviewee to comment on any other issues that you may have missed. You can also send out a questionnaire to people to obtain their views, but you will obviously tend to obtain more information on a one-to-one basis. And at this stage of a project you will want to obtain some real detailed feedback.

To carry out your review, you will need to:

- plan what information you need to gather
- conduct your interviews
- present the review report to your client.

PLANNING WHAT INFORMATION TO GATHER

A successful review will need careful planning, as there are a number of steps that you need to carry out. These are:

- deciding who you should interview
- preparing questions for the interviews

- arrange interview appointments
- preparing your review report.

You should aim to complete a review process within one month. This should include your interviews, documenting them, analysing results, preparing a report and presenting the report to your client.

Deciding who you should interview

The answer to this question will be governed by the type of assignment you have carried out and the amount of time you have available to devote to the review. For example, if you were project managing the launch of a new IT system to a number of different organization sites, then you might aim to interview a representative sample of users of the new system, the team who built it, information providers, and your key clients. Where applicable, your review should also extend to members of any steering committee and departments that may have been supporting the project. This might potentially involve at least seven meetings and several more depending on the number of interviewees involved from each interested group. If there were several hundred final users of the system, you would probably want to select a small group of users representing a geographical area, be it nationally or internationally. You might also include departments who provide regular information to the new system, such as personnel, marketing, financial control, customer services and production. The people who built the system – the system developers – might include a mixture of both internal and external resources and again you would probably want to check their views. So very quickly, you might have between twenty and thirty interviews to complete. On very large and complex projects involving high levels of expenditure and major operational changes, you may well be required to carry out this size of review, as clients will be looking to identify real and tangible results.

Conversely, if you were responsible for organizing an

annual management forum, then the number of interviews would be significantly less. But even in this case you should aim to interview a cross-section of delegates, your client and a representative sample of any external parties who may have participated in the conference.

Will your client sanction a budget to carry out a review? On large-scale projects there will probably be a strong expectation that a full review will take place, but you may need to work hard at persuading your client to fund a review on smaller projects. Much will depend on the circumstances surrounding the original project, and in some instances you may need to conduct a review of your time and commitment. Where client assistance is not forthcoming, avoid the temptation to forget about a review as they are vital to your future marketing efforts and can convince new clients of your capabilities and of the benefits of using your services. Don't miss this important opportunity to document and sell the impact of your work.

Preparing questions for the interview

A range of questions are presented in this chapter for you to consider and use when structuring your review. Alternatively, you can use the forms in the toolkit chapter to conduct your review. Use the appropriate form for the type of information you will be gathering according to the model presented in Figure 7.2. These forms include the following:

Consultant assessment:
- Self – Internal consultant's self assessment form
- By client – Client's satisfaction assessment form
- By project team or customer – Internal consultant performance assessment form

Project related:
- Project effectiveness – Project review form

- Process effectiveness (IT system) – New system operation review form
- Process effectiveness – New process review form
- Customer satisfaction – New process review or New system operation review form
- Additional requests – Problem identification form
- Additional requests – Request for additional improvements form.

INSIGHT

If you are pressed for time, select the appropriate interview forms from the toolkit chapter and use these for gathering information from your interviews.

Arranging interview appointments

After you have identified the people you wish to interview, arrange the appointments through your client's office. Find out where the people you are going to interview are located and make allowances for travelling to their offices. If they are located abroad, you will need to make provision for obtaining any necessary travel approvals. As an alternative, you may find it easier to ask if they would be willing to travel to your office or your client's office. Finally, if most people are located in one building, don't be tempted into interviewing too many people in one day. Your capacity to remain alert and focused will diminish as the day progresses. Plan for a maximum of four/five interviews a day lasting about one hour each, and give yourself about half an hour between interviews to make final notes or to prepare before the next interview.

Planning your review report

At this stage you must allocate enough of your time to prepare your final report. You will now have a good idea of who you will interview, and you should allocate at least two hours per person for writing up your interview notes.

CONDUCTING INTERVIEWS

Always go into any review meeting extremely well prepared! Think carefully beforehand about the type of questions you will want to ask. Use the forms presented in the toolkit chapter to assist you in the process.

When the interview begins, make sure that you inform the interviewee that your review is intended to measure the impact of your work and that he or she is not being assessed in any way. Relax the interviewee by discussing the background to the assignment, your involvement and who your client is. Let him or her know that your client will be circulating the review report to all those who participated in it. Before you begin with your questions, let him or her know that you will be noting down his or her responses. Do not hide your notes, and tell the interviewee that he or she can inspect them at any time during the interview.

Third party reviews

You need to be aware that you may not be the only person carrying out a review, as your client may want an independent third party to conduct an assessment. If another person, either within the organization or from outside, has been asked to carry out a review, you need to meet and discuss their structure for conducting the review. If you are also going to carry out a review, then try to avoid interviewing the same people twice. Your credibility, and possibly that of the assignment, may suffer from this needless duplication. If two reviews are being conducted, discuss both your aims and questions. Understand the background from the other person's point of view and try to agree a joint timetable for interviewing and completing both reviews so as to minimize disruption.

Evaluating your own performance

As an internal consultant, you need to know what aspects of your assistance have been successful or not. You must validate the impact of your consulting efforts. You also need to identify to what extent other organizational factors have influenced the outcomes of the project. Without this information, neither you nor your client will be clear about how to manage similar situations in the future.

Yourself: assessing your own performance

Here is a list of questions you can ask yourself to assess your own performance on a project. You do not need to answer them all, but use those most appropriate for the assignment on which you were working:

- Were the assignment objectives achieved?
- Has your client's problem been solved or addressed?
- What could you have done differently to improve the final result?
- What do your colleagues feel about the results of the project?
- How do your client's staff regard your involvement?
- How good is your current client relationship?
- Will your client recommend you to their colleagues?
- Has your client asked you to undertake additional work for them?
- Did the assignment or project stay within budget?

Other people's assessment of your performance

You also need to understand how other people and groups who participated in the assignment regarded your performance. Remember, you can ask the same set of questions to a cross-section of people who were actively involved in the project.

- To what extent do you think the internal consultant contributed to meeting the assignment's objectives?
- What specific actions taken by the internal consultant helped to meet the assignment objectives?
- What specific actions taken by the internal consultant hindered you in meeting the assignment objectives?
- What might the internal consultant have done (but did not) that might have helped you to meet the assignment objectives?
- Would you use the internal consultant to help you address a similar situation in the future?
- What has the consultant left of their skills in your organization for you or your staff to utilize in the future?
- Would you choose to work with the consultant again in the future?
- Would you recommend the internal consultant to colleagues with similar problems or issues?
- Would you say that the internal consultant helped you significantly?

Assessing customer satisfaction of a new system

If your assignment has resulted in a new system being implemented, such as a new accounting system, then you need to assess people's satisfaction with the changes and the way they were implemented. You may identify two groups of people, such as those who are involved in operating the new system and those who receive information from it. You might arrange to interview one person who will represent the views of each group. In many cases you may have to interview several people from each group to get a balanced view. This process is usual when the project has involved people from different departments such as marketing, production or personnel. All these people may derive benefit from or use the new system, but they may have very different views on its effectiveness. You are looking to assess their satisfaction in either using or obtaining information from the new system. Consider using some of the following questions:

- Has the system delivered new benefits to the people who use it?
- Have all the expected benefits been achieved?
- Is the new system easy to operate?
- Are jobs easier to do with the new system?
- Have the business objectives been met?
- Did the internal consultant involve people sufficiently during the project?
- Did the internal consultant keep people informed of progress?
- Is the documentation supporting the new system satisfactory?

Reviewing a new system or procedure

In some cases you will also want to determine the effectiveness of any new system or procedure. Here are some questions you may ask if a new procedure has been implemented, such as a new ordering process:

- Have the original problems been addressed?
- What do you like about the new procedure and why?
- What don't you like about the new procedure and why?
- Will this new process make your job easier to do?
- Is the procedure quicker than the previous one?

For a new systems implementation, such as a sales monitoring system, you might use the following questions:

- Is the system easy to use?
- Are the response times fast enough?
- What do you like about the new system and why?

- What don't you like about the new system and why?
- If things go wrong, is there a contingency procedure?
- If the contingency procedure was used, was it effective?
- If information is stored on the new system, is it secure?

Identifying continuing problem areas

You may also need to identify any continuing problems being experienced by people as a result of the implementation. Here are a few questions you might ask:

- Have you been experiencing any further problems since the work was implemented?
- When did they start to occur?
- What do you feel is contributing to these problems?
- What actions have you taken so far to address these issues?
- Have you reported these problems to anyone else?
- Do you have any thoughts as to how the problem might be dealt with?

Reviewing your project process

In any project you should aim to review your project management process. This will help you and your client to identify successful practices and also improvements for any future projects. So consider using the following questions:

- What practices helped to make the project go smoothly?
- What should we avoid doing during future projects?
- What difficulties did you encounter while the work was being carried out?
- What did you like about the work plan?

- What else helped to make the project run smoothly?
- Why do you think we had that problem with x?
- What other groups do you think assisted the development of the project?
- What groups or departments hindered development?

Gathering recommendations for additional improvements

Although a new system may have been in place only for a short time before you carry out your review, nevertheless it is likely that requests for further changes will be made. Apart from recording them, your review report can also impress on your client the need for a process to manage these requests for change. The dividing line between the end of your original assignment and further improvements and enhancements can often be blurred, and a review will help to define this divide and bring to your client's attention any outstanding issues.

For now, though, you only need to include some of the following questions in your report:

- What changes do you want to the new system?
- How can the new system be improved?
- How can the operation of the system be improved?
- What changes would you recommend to further increase the business benefit?

PRESENTING THE REVIEW REPORT

After you have completed all your interviews, you need to review your notes and identify the main messages that emerge. In preparing your client report, provide a brief background to the project and its objectives from your terms of reference. Also indicate who you interviewed and their departments. Then detail the main learning points you have identified. Try to address any problem areas as well as the successes. The chances are that if you ignore something by not referring to it in your report, your client will pick it up by some other means. This only makes you look devious. So be honest and deal with difficult issues up front. Most clients will respect your honesty and integrity.

As this type of report can be expected to be circulated to a number of other people in your organization, as well as those who contributed to the review, prepare a summary page of the key messages and results. In your presentation and covering letter to your client, do not forget to highlight your main achievements on the project. Remember, you must be thinking about the next project and future opportunities, so make sure that your client is aware of your successful input.

Finally, you must indicate to your client that you are seeking agreement to formally close the project on the basis that it has been satisfactorily completed. So get a written confirmation to signal the end of a project. Remember, never allow your projects to drift on endlessly. You will have other clients who will need your time and energy.

The main headings to include in your report are:

- Review summary
- Project background
- Project objectives
- Consultant assessment
- Project review.

At this stage you are formally ending your consulting cycle with a successful project result and a happy client who feels positive about working with you. Thus you have laid solid foundations for your next project.

REVIEWING AND EXITING PROJECTS: BEING CLIENT FOCUSED

This final stage of the client project involves establishing whether your project's objectives were achieved and formally 'signing off' your involvement in a project.

Questions you might ask

- Have you signalled earlier the end of the project/ assignment with your client, thus avoiding any surprises?
- Have you agreed a project end date with your client?
- Is there to be a formal hand-over of the project to your client?
- Is your client comfortable with the close of the project?
- Are there any major issues still outstanding that are worrying your client?
- Have you secured the views of all the relevant parties?
- Have you been sufficiently rigorous in your review process?
- Have you been open and honest about any problem areas?

Client's perspective of you

- Have you given me ample notice of the project's conclusion?
- Have you fulfilled the terms of reference?
- Have I enjoyed working with you?
- Would I want to work with you again?
- Have you left a positive impression on my team?
- Were you always open, honest and direct in your dealings?

Other statements/questions you might use

- We would like to have a final meeting to conclude and review our work.

- Are you happy with everything?

- Are there any outstanding issues?

- We believe that signifies the conclusion of the work plan and the project itself.

- Is there anything we did not do that would have helped the project?

- We could do that, but it would require us to devote additional resources because the project timetable has been completed.

- We do not have sufficient time/resources to take on that additional workload.

- We would be pleased to assist you on that additional work.

- We have enjoyed working on this project with you.

8 Presenting client feedback

PRESENTING CLIENT FEEDBACK

'Always ask yourself the question – would I be happy to stand in the shoes of my client whose career prospects will be dependent on implementing my recommendations?'

Mike Gelder, Divisional Manager, Lloyds Bank

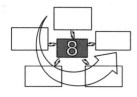

A vital and ongoing part of any consulting process involves providing your client with continuous feedback concerning the progress of their project. Being proactive and keeping your client up-to-date concerning developments and problem areas is fundamental to you becoming a successful consultant. On large and complex projects, client feedback will take place on an almost daily basis. But in every consulting project, regardless of size, there will be structured phases of client feedback which follow the key milestones on your project timetable.

When giving client feedback at any reporting stage, you must be operating to the best of your ability. These situations are where the stakes are highest, with your client looking to assess your capability and professionalism. At the same time, you will be aiming to secure your client's commitment to any of your findings or proposals. So it is crucial that you manage feedback in a skilled and effective manner. You must lead your client through a logical analysis and at the same time deal with any issues or problems that might arise. In most cases this demands that you pre-empt difficult questions and foresee issues that may be preoccupying your client. When you manage feedback in a professional manner, your client will not only feel comfortable with the quality of your work but also develop greater personal confidence in working with you.

Of course, when meeting clients on a regular basis you

should aim to utilize many of the skills outlined in our interviewing section, but the two formal elements of presenting client feedback involve

- Report writing
- Making presentations.

Both of these activities have to be mastered by the internal consultant. In the following sections we provide an essential guide to the do's and don'ts.

INTRODUCTION TO REPORT WRITING

The ability to communicate effectively in writing is a skill that you must master as an internal consultant. A project report is often your major deliverable to a client, and clients tend to view reports as major evidence of your ability and success in tackling an assignment. As well as supporting your future involvement in any implementation or follow-up work, a well-written report is also a major marketing opportunity.

Client reports have two fundamental objectives:

- To provide information that informs or educates your client on a particular problem
- To influence or persuade your client towards a particular view and form of action.

The advantages of written reports are that they can:

- provide documentary proof and a formal record of your work
- impose strong disciplines in planning and structuring your work plan as well as your final report structure
- allow your client time to reflect on your work
- be structured to communicate to different levels of client
- focus your client on the critical issues and actions
- be an efficient method of communicating the outcomes of your work to a wider client audience.

The disadvantages of reports are that they can be:

- expensive in terms of time and cost
- liable to client misinterpretation
- abused by clients or others through selective editing or quoting out of context
- a client substitute for taking action
- ineffective unless accompanied by a strong supporting presentation
- prone to not being fully read by your clients.

A consultant's report can communicate authority if it is well structured and written with clarity. Badly written reports destroy the credibility of your work and recommendations. A report will only generate an appropriate client response if your original terms of reference have been fully met and you have managed your client's expectations as to your final report's content and structure. An effective client report should therefore describe:

- what you set out to do for the client
- what you have done
- what you think ought to be done in the future
- the reasons why your recommendations should be implemented.

A good consultant report should also:

- provide a permanent record of the work undertaken
- list improvement actions
- avoid misunderstandings (bearing in mind that clients sometimes hear what they want to hear)
- confirm client/consultant agreements
- focus attention and clarify major issues
- influence your client's thinking
- secure client agreement and action.

INSIGHT

An excellent test of the clarity of any report is that it can be understood at a first reading by anyone who does not have a detailed understanding of the project or problems under review. So give your initial drafts to someone who has had no involvement in the project and get his or her reaction. Ask him or her if it makes sense.

Different types of client report

Persuasive: This type of report is commonly used by consultants in trying to initiate change. It aims to persuade a client to adopt a particular approach or plan.

Instructive: This report advises clients how to do something specific, e.g. to introduce a new system or process.

Investigative: The investigative report is simply a statement of facts. For example, you may be asked to provide the results of a survey, in which case you might simply report the results with no other interpretation being provided.

Getting your report structure right

The starting point for structuring your report is to begin with a review of your broad findings, conclusions and recommendations. These areas define the broad content of your report. You will then need to consider:

- dividing your report into major sections of your project, e.g. management reporting, production, IT, etc.

- reviewing each section in turn. Describing the present situation, key findings, recommended changes and future actions for each section

- distinguishing between the major and minor points of the key areas. Any minor points are best covered in an appendix to avoid cluttering the main body of your report. Also avoid too much cross-referencing. Always aim for a balance between your main text and appendices

- presenting a logical flow in your analysis and linking the various sections effectively.

A typical report structure

Introduction

This should give the background to the project and the circumstances under which you initially met your client to discuss matters.

Scope of the assignment

This section should describe the areas under review and any limitations which surrounded your work. You should list your project timetable, the sources from which you obtained information and detail the response rates to any questionnaires.

Summary of conclusions and recommendations

This is your executive summary intended for busy readers who wish to obtain a quick and focused overview of your report. It should therefore be written in a bullet point format. Your conclusions should be listed logically and cross-referenced to any recommendations.

Present situation

This describes the current situation and refers to any weaknesses where appropriate. It is important not to assume that your client is aware of or understands the present situation. An unbiased and well-written description of the current situation can be enormously helpful for a client, as it helps to sharpen their thoughts and ideas. So once again, be wary of making any assumptions.

Detailed recommendations

Your recommendations must follow on logically from your conclusions and should contain no flaws of logic in your analysis. Every recommendation must be linked to one or more of your conclusions. In turn, you need to provide as much detail as possible in your recommendations.

Implementation actions

It is no good telling a client that they need an IT strategy review if they have no idea how to go about it. Your implementation section must provide a clear road map to help your client see the way ahead. Your recommendations need to state:

- who should take action
- what action is required
- when action should be taken
- how long the action will take to implement
- what the benefits of the action will be
- what costs are involved.

Your assistance

This is the sales element of the report. It should build on the main body of your report, so that your suggested involvement in follow-up work comes as no surprise to your client.

Closing paragraph

Thank the client and their staff for their co-operation and help during the project.

Appendices

Appendices contain those details and facts which would otherwise clutter the main body and message of your report. They do, however, need to be included, as they provide further support for your work and findings.

How to start writing a client report

'Keep it simple. Put one page of paper on your client's desk and you will get a response.'

Alan Goodson, Research and Development, Dow Chemicals

A common challenge in writing client reports is that you need to be very selective in your choice of final content. Too much detail or too many facts may cause confusion. Too little may create doubt about your whole approach and analysis. As a consultant, when you begin to write a report you will invariably have too much information. You will not normally include every bit of information you have collected, as this will lead to a lengthy report. Over-lengthy reports that are packed with endless detail are more liable to frustrate and irritate then actually please your client.

You will find it helpful to list all the topic areas and data that you consider relevant to the report. Try to do this without any pre-judgement about the suitability of the information. At this stage you should not worry about duplication. Once you have listed all the information, you can begin the process of sifting for duplication and begin eliminating data. The next step is to begin linking pieces of information into themes and topic areas. At that stage you should have a good basis on which to begin shaping the content of your report.

You will need to select information and facts that are relevant to your main conclusions and recommendations. At the same time, you will need to avoid information which is capable of creating client confusion or is based on gossip or erroneous facts.

When writing a client report, be clear about its purpose and objectives. You can actually start this process at the very beginning of a project by:

- examining your terms of reference
- identifying the areas you are going to focus on
- formulating some idea of what your final report structure will look like.

You should also try to develop and write the key sections of your report as your project progresses. In the final stages, allow plenty of time to write and produce your report, e.g. for a 30-page report allow a minimum of three days and have at the back of your mind that it is more likely to be five days. Also allow sufficient time to have your report read and edited by your colleagues.

You will also need to:

- reflect on your client(s) and their colleagues' perspectives on the issues. What are their relative positions in the organization and to what extent do they agree or disagree about the problems and any possible solutions? Are they supportive or hostile? Will anyone that you have to report to be starting with a biased or negative view?

- consider whether the eventual readers of your report will have a detailed knowledge of the issues involved. If not, you will need to bring them up-to-date in your report's overview

- establish and agree the final distribution of the report

- lead your client through the report with a reasoned and logical analysis

- deal with any contentious issues in your report by using strong logic and fact-based arguments

- predict and deal with any possible questions that might come from your client

- consider your client's underlying motivation and needs in attempting to solve the problem. Are you really addressing these fundamental points?

- keep in focus the key decision maker(s) among your client's team

- consider any actions or agreements you require from your client. For example, you may want your client's agreement to continue funding additional research or to involve some specialist input. If so, it will be important to deal with areas such as the reasons for carrying out this additional work, the benefits, timescales and costs that might accrue

- find out whether your client will subsequently have to sell your report's proposals to their boss. If so, you need to help your client with this task

- clearly state how your client can action any recommendations
- indicate and promote your possible involvement in any additional follow-on work.

Other practical tips on writing client reports

- Use simple and plain language throughout your report. Never use a long word where a short word means the same thing
- Keep your sentences short. If a sentence works without a word, cut it out
- Try to avoid technical terms and unnecessary jargon. If jargon is required, you must ensure that the terms are defined and explained. If an everyday phrase is available, use it instead of any buzz words
- Use the active tense rather than the passive – 'service levels have been improved' is preferable to 'an improvement in service levels has been made'
- Support your arguments with facts
- Make sure that you have clear and logical conclusions and recommendations.

INSIGHT

A very powerful way to build up your report structure is to use the classic discipline of:

- Findings
- Conclusions
- Recommendations.

The process is to link all your findings to your conclusions and in turn your recommendations to your conclusions. This should enable you to develop a strong pattern of logic. You should not then find yourself in a position where you are presenting recommendations which are not linked to your conclusions or, even worse, presenting conclusions for which you have no real findings.

You can remember this approach by recalling the following statements:

We found. . . .
On the basis of those findings we therefore conclude. . . .
And on the basis of those conclusions we are therefore recommending. . . .

This should then enable you to draw up a strong case and argument that will withstand your client's review. See Figure 8.1.

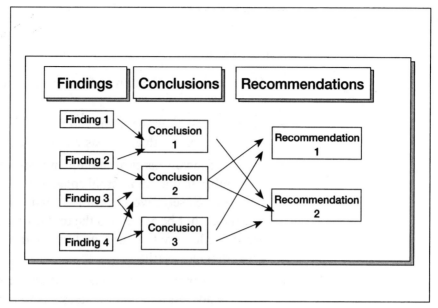

Figure 8.1 *Process for building your report – link findings into conclusions and then into recommendations*

INSIGHT

Remember, if people want to attack you or your recommendations they will look to criticize your analysis. So if you are recommending actions for which you do not have any findings or conclusions, you need to do some more information gathering.

On the logistics side, remember to:

- try to make one person responsible for producing the final report. Reports that are written by committees or groups of people generally prove ineffective and seldom produce results, as the collective process tends to sanitize any significant points or actions
- check the availability of your word processing resources
- agree how and when you are going to distribute the report to your client
- check that your client will be available when the final document is ready
- alert your client to any possible delays sooner rather than later.

Reviewing reports

Below are some questions for you to consider when reviewing your report.

- Have we fulfilled the terms of reference? If not, why not?

- Have we described the scope and methods of our work and dealt with any areas we did not cover?

- Are our conclusions clear and unambiguous? Remember that as an internal consultant you will have been closely involved with the assignment – issues may not be as clear to the reader of your report as they are to you. If in doubt, redraft areas that lack clarity

- Are our recommendations clear and unambiguous? Do they address all of our conclusions?

- Is the report summary consistent with the main body of our report?

- Does the content of each section contain material that is consistent with the heading?

- Are the content, wording and style of the report appropriate to our client's needs?

- Have we used any loose language that might be prone to misinterpretation by our clients? Look out for emotive phrases or language, as these can always generate strong client reactions. If present, review them and remove them from your final draft if appropriate

- Have we alerted our client to any possible surprises in advance?

- Have we left out any important issues or facts?

- Who can we get to play 'devil's advocate' in questioning any 'grey areas' in the report?

- Is the tone of our report constructive and positive or negative and depressing?

Finally, there are some detailed points of housekeeping that are always worth a final check when reviewing your final report:

- Check your contents page against the text
- Check the paragraph and appendix cross-references
- Check the names and titles of all client personnel
- Check your section headings and sub-headings, particularly against the contents page
- Are all cross-references present and correct?
- Similarly, check any appendix headings against your contents page
- Finally, ensure that the typing, printing and collation of your final report are double-checked. Simple but silly mistakes at this stage can destroy an otherwise excellent piece of work.

MAKING CLIENT PRESENTATIONS

Making presentations is a difficult but essential activity for any internal consultant. You must be able to present information in a professional manner so that your client understands, accepts and actions your proposals and recommendations. As an internal consultant, you may have completed some high-quality research and analysis, but all your efforts will be wasted unless you can influence your client and their colleagues in a formal presentation.

As the development of presentation media continues to become more sophisticated, so too are your clients expecting higher standards. Your presentational skills and messages need to exceed your client expectations. It is important to remember that the vast majority of presentations are more often remembered for the presenter than their content. As an internal consultant, you cannot afford to under-estimate this part of the role.

Preparing client presentations

The first essential element in preparing any presentation is to consider your client's position and recognize that they are important and will want to be respected. You must also reflect on their individual needs and objectives and the extent to which you have to satisfy them. You can do this by asking yourself the following questions:

- What have you discovered?
- Are you focusing on the real issues?
- Will your findings, proposals and recommendations help your client?
- What are the problems your client needs to address?
- Are your recommendations saving or costing your client money?
- Are you improving the efficiency of their operation?
- What does your client need to do about the issues?
- What options do they have available?
- Are they going to want to continue working with you?

Having addressed these questions, you must then decide on your own objectives for the presentation. You need to consider whether you are asking for your client's confirmation and agreement or whether you are trying to secure additional resources for the project. Answering these questions will help you to focus further on the structure and detail of your presentation.

In developing your presentation structure, make sure that it has three parts:

- A clear beginning, involving an introduction and background overview to the project
- A strong middle section, which details your analysis
- A sound conclusion, which comprises a summary and some clear suggestions for action.

You also need to consider the overall timing for your

presentation and each section within it. Also remember to find out well in advance:

- where the presentation will take place
- who will be in the audience
- how much time you will have.

In deciding on the content of your presentation, ask yourself:

- What benefits am I offering my client?
- How do I propose to deal with any difficult or contentious issues?
- How will I involve the client during the presentation?
- What are likely to be my client's critical questions/ objections?
- What actions will my client need to take at the end of my presentation?

INSIGHT

Avoid being the expert and talking too much at your client. Always structure your presentation so that your client is invited to comment on it at an early stage. You must get an early reaction to what you are saying. Plan a pause in your presentation after 20–25 minutes and invite client reaction. You don't want to discover at the end of a long presentation that your client totally disagrees with what you have presented. Early feedback means that you can adjust the content sooner rather than later.

Presentation media

In selecting the media to make your presentation, you need to address the following questions:

- How do you propose to communicate your key points and messages? (description, analogy, facts, graphics, examples, competitive data, etc.)
- What visual aids or media will best communicate the points you wish to make?
  - Overhead projector
  - Computer projection
  - 35-millimetre slides
  - Flipcharts
  - Slide book

- Practical demonstration
- Video.

Also consider the room setting that you are going to be using and the logistics involved in employing different forms of media. Remember, using complex equipment can increase the chances of technical breakdowns. Also it is possible that by using overly sophisticated media you may lose the clarity of your message. Consider the size of client group that will be present. What kind of atmosphere do you want to create – formal, informal, relaxed, sophisticated, authoritative? All these issues involve the process side of your presentation, and you need carefully to consider all these questions when preparing a client presentation. Do not assume that just because you have done a great piece of analysis that is the end of the job and that the report will sell itself. You have to influence your client, and this is where your understanding of the processes involved in presenting come into play.

Delivering your presentation

After having planned the structure and content of your presentation, you then have to do the difficult part, which is to present it to your client in an authoritative and influential manner. As with many of the other skills involved in internal consultancy, you can only develop real expertise in giving presentations through continuous practice and experience. Below are some of the essential do's and don'ts:

- Make sure that you rehearse and practise. Don't wait to find out until the actual day whether your presentation works or not A serious rehearsal will usually reveal any weak areas in your presentation and provide you with ample opportunity to make any changes or adjustments. You can find out whether all elements of your presentation work by going through the session in some detail. If in doubt, get a colleague to sit in on the practice session. Ask him or her to be very critical. Fine-tuning at this low-risk stage is better than on the actual day

- Anticipate what questions will be asked, including the obvious, difficult and 'unthinkable'. A key part of your planning is thinking up the really awkward questions that will be asked
- Stand up straight and project confidence
- Vary your body posture, but don't wander around in a way that will distract your client from what you are saying
- Avoid fidgeting and the 'classic rattling of coins and keys in your pocket'
- Speak in a slow but clear and pronounced fashion

INSIGHT

Remember, always try to make your client feel strong, not weak. Clients do not want to hear that they are no good. So concentrate on motivating your client. This does not mean avoiding difficult issues, but recognize the fact that your client may have been experiencing difficult circumstances.

Give clients credit wherever possible, and try not to slip into critical or patronizing statements. The fact is that in some situations it may indeed look all bad, but you still have to find something positive to report. Any client who has to listen to a presentation that has nothing positive to say is likely to become an unhappy client. Your job is to make them feel strong!

- Project authority in your voice. A hesitant and mumbling delivery will irritate your audience and destroy your credibility
  - Vary your sentence length
  - Vary the pitch, tone and pace of your voice to match your presentation
  - Use facial expressions that match your presentation content – smile at humour and try to demonstrate surprise at an important finding or key issue
  - Use hand gestures to emphasize key points
- In your introduction provide a brief background to the project and highlight your original terms of reference. This brings everyone up to speed. This is important because you may have some people

who are intimately involved with the project and others who are somewhat remote

- Have a powerful opening statement. A strong reference to the fundamental objectives of the project can be a good way of focusing everyone's attention. Try using, for example:
  - 'Before we begin, ladies and gentlemen, let us just remind ourselves why we are here. . . .'
  - To then follow this opening with a hard business issue such as reducing costs or increasing sales will generally get your client's attention

- If reporting back on the results of interviews, preserve any previous confidentiality agreements with interviewees by reminding your client of these assurances. This helps you to avoid any pointed questions, such as 'Who said that?', which might come later in your presentation

- Speak the language of your business or organization. Do not clutter your presentation with esoteric jargon. Keep it simple and business relevant

- Look directly at all your clients and remember constantly to scan your audience rather than stare at or focus on key individuals. There is always a temptation to maintain eye contact with people who are showing positive signs of interest. Remember, there are other people present and you should also be trying to gauge their reaction to what you are saying. You need to identify whether they seem unhappy or surprised at what you are saying

- Make sure that you summarize before, during and after each key stage of your presentation. If you are working and presenting as a consulting team, make sure that you introduce each speaker before he or she begins. We call this 'sign-posting' – it helps tell your client where you are taking them and identifies where they have been

INSIGHT

When making a client presentation, try to use 'we' rather than 'you'. It is always easy to slip into a telling mode when giving a presentation, and bad consultants start saying things like:

- **You have some major problems here**
- **You need to tackle these issues**
- **You must address this problem.**

To a client this can sound very irritating and condescending. Remember, you are on the same side, so always use 'we' rather than 'you'. It helps develop rapport and sounds significantly better to your client.

Similarly, use 'challenges', not 'problems'. Stating that 'we have some major challenges' is far better than saying 'you have some major problems'. So try to keep your language positive.

- Enliven your presentation by the use of appropriate comments or quotes which you picked up during the course of your research. A simple but insightful quote, to illustrate some statistical or graphical point can be ten times more powerful. But do remember to safeguard confidentiality. So, if necessary, make the quote anonymous except for a job title or role
- Watch for individual client responses as your presentation develops
- Nodding heads or frowns should be picked up on by reflecting questions back to the client:
  - 'You seem a little unhappy with that last point? Have we missed something?'
  - 'Is that finding an issue for you?'
- Pace your presentation so that it gathers momentum from beginning to end.

If you are presenting options to your client, use a simple cost–benefit approach to focus your client's thoughts. Simply using a high, medium and low rating can add considerably to any subsequent debate, and will help develop your client's commitment to any eventual selection decision. Figure 8.2 illustrates this simple but powerful approach.

- Don't 'fade away' towards the end of your presentation. Make sure that you have a strong finish
- Allow ample time for discussion at the end of your presentation. Engaging your client is critical,

Options	Costs of implementation	Benefit to organization	Practicality/ease of implementation
A	**High**	**Low**	**Difficult**
B			
C			
D			

Figure 8.2   *Presenting your client with implementation options*

so make sure that you allow sufficient time to discuss the issues that have been raised

● Remember to be enthusiastic and confident. If you are not seen to be convinced, your clients will never be!

INSIGHT

When rehearsing your presentation, invite someone in to listen who has not had any involvement in the project. He or she will be able to critique your presentation in a powerful way, not having any emotional involvement in the project. You may discover that he or she raises some interesting points or questions which you have overlooked.

PRESENTING CLIENT FEEDBACK: BEING CLIENT FOCUSED

'Communicate bad news early – never cover up!'

Tony Edgar, Business Manager, Lloyds Bank

This consultancy stage involves you presenting feedback to your client throughout a project life cycle. It also involves making specific presentations and writing key reports, particularly towards the end of a project.

Questions you should ask

- Is your analysis rigorous, accurate and clear?
- Can you support your findings, conclusions and recommendations?
- Will your findings and recommendations help your client?
- Will your client respond positively or negatively to your feedback?
- Have you managed your client's expectations in advance of your feedback presentation?
- Is your feedback presentation in the right format, style and level of detail?
- Have you spent enough time rehearsing your presentation?
- Have you thought of all the 'unthinkable' questions?
- Have you adequately planned how to move your client forward to the next stage of the project?
- How will you report back to interviewees who helped you during the information gathering phase of your work?

Client's perspective of you

- How valid is your feedback?
- How thorough has your work been?
- Have you upset anyone during your work?

- Do I understand, accept and agree with the findings or results?
- How will my colleagues react to your findings and recommendations?
- How well have you managed the feedback process?
- Have you dealt adequately with my questions and concerns?
- Have you added to my understanding of the issues and problems?
- Do your recommendations represent a solution to the problem?

Other client thoughts:

- So what conclusions have you produced?
- I can't believe that is actually happening.
- I would like to get a quick overview of your findings.
- I would like to spend more time examining this issue.
- Who said that? It's rubbish, it can't be true!
- How have you come to that conclusion?
- You found that people thought . . .?
- I am startled to be told that. . . .
- Was there anything positive that you discovered?
- It's all pretty bad news.
- Are we doing anything well?
- OK, what do we need to do next?
- I can't help thinking you have missed something there.
- I think you may have misinterpreted that point.
- That cannot be true.
- I tend to agree with that.
- Yes, that is interesting.
- I would like to comment on that.

Other statements/questions you might use

- There were some positive as well as negative issues emerging from our investigation.
- We would like to provide you with an overview of our findings and then focus on some specific issues.
- We are not sure about this specific point, but we think what is happening here is. . . .
- We would welcome your reactions to these points.
- You may disagree, but the results *do* indicate a strong negative perception about this issue.
- Perhaps we need to get additional information about that question.
- This point is certainly reinforced by section ten of our report.
- We will cover those points later on in our presentation.
- Perhaps I could cover that at the end of our presentation.

9 The internal consultant's toolkit

THE CONSULTANT'S TOOLKIT

Throughout this book we have stressed the need to actively manage your client relationships and made many references to using a number of forms to assist you in this process. On the following pages we have outlined a series of template forms that you might like to use or adapt to help you in managing your clients and projects. They cover the key elements of our internal consultant management process.

INITIAL MEETING FORM

Date/Time	Location

Dept Name/Present

Meeting Purpose

What is the client reporting structure?	Description of client's operation

What are your client's issues?	Initial thoughts to solve problem

Action	Next meeting date/time/place
	Duration of meeting

TERMS OF REFERENCE FORM - Page 1 of 3

Client Name	Date
Consultant Name	Location
Project Name	Start Date

Background

Objective

Boundary

TERMS OF REFERENCE FORM - Page 2 of 3

Constraints

Assumptions

Reporting

Deliverables and milestones

TERMS OF REFERENCE FORM - Page 3 of 3

Activity Time Chart for Project

Activity	Who	Effort	Start	Week 1 2 3 4 5 6 7 8
		TOTAL Effort:	days	

Estimated Costs

Resource Name:	Rate:	Effort:	Cost:
Resource Name:	Rate:	Effort:	Cost:
Resource Name:	Rate:	Effort:	Cost:
Resource Name:	Rate:	Effort:	Cost:
Equipment Name:			Cost:
Equipment Name:			Cost:
Expenses:			Cost:

Total Estimated Costs:

Approved by Client: _____

Date: _____

INTERNAL CONSULTANT'S SELF-ASSESSMENT FORM

Consultant Name	Date

Assignment Name

Have project objectives been achieved?

1. Fully ☐ Partially ☐ Not ☐
2. Fully ☐ Partially ☐ Not ☐
3. Fully ☐ Partially ☐ Not ☐
4. Fully ☐ Partially ☐ Not ☐

Why have objectives not been achieved?

1.
2.
3.
4.

What could I have done differently to improve the final result?

Was the project completed?

On time: Yes ☐ No ☐ Why?

In budget: Yes ☐ No ☐ Why?

I think at the end of the project

My client relationship is:	Good ☐	Fair ☐	Poor ☐
My relationship with the client's staff is:	Good ☐	Fair ☐	Poor ☐
My fellow consultants rate my work as:	Good ☐	Fair ☐	Poor ☐
My client rates my work as:	Good ☐	Fair ☐	Poor ☐
My client rates my project management skills as:	Good ☐	Fair ☐	Poor ☐

CLIENT'S SATISFACTION ASSESSMENT FORM

Client Name	Location
Assessor Name	Date

Project Name

What new benefits has the project given you?

What benefits should have been delivered?

What did you like during the development of the project?

What didn't you like during the development of the project?

Was the assignment effectively controlled to keep it

On time: Yes ☐   No ☐   Why?

In budget: Yes ☐   No ☐   Why?

I think

The new system/procedure is easy to use:	Yes ☐	n/a ☐	No ☐
My role is easier to conduct using the new system:	Yes ☐	n/a ☐	No ☐
The internal consultant involved me during development:	Yes ☐	n/a ☐	No ☐
The internal consultant kept me well informed:	Yes ☐	n/a ☐	No ☐
The documentation for the system/procedure is good:	Yes ☐	n/a ☐	No ☐

INTERNAL CONSULTANT PERFORMANCE ASSESSMENT

Assessor Name	Location
Consultant Name	Date

Project Name

How much has the consultant contributed to meeting the project objectives?

1.   A lot ☐   Some ☐   Little ☐
2.   A lot ☐   Some ☐   Little ☐
3.   A lot ☐   Some ☐   Little ☐
4.   A lot ☐   Some ☐   Little ☐

What specific actions did the consultant take to meet these objectives?

1.
2.
3.
4.

What did you like about the consultant's method of operating?

What did you dislike about the consultant's method of operating?

Did the consultant control the assignment to keep it

On time: Yes ☐   No ☐   Why?
In budget: Yes ☐   No ☐   Why?

I think

I would use this consultant again:	Yes ☐	Possibly ☐	No ☐
The consultant left valuable skills in the organization:	Yes ☐	Possibly ☐	No ☐
I would recommend this consultant to my colleagues:	Yes ☐	Possibly ☐	No ☐
The consultant has significantly helped me:	Yes ☐	Possibly ☐	No ☐
The consultant worked well with my team:	Yes ☐	Possibly ☐	No ☐

PROJECT REVIEW FORM

Interviewee Name	Location
Assessor Name	Date

Project Name

What were the best practices in this project that we should use in future?

What should we avoid doing in future projects?

Which groups were helpful during this project and how?

Which groups were not helpful during this project and how?

NEW SYSTEM OPERATION REVIEW FORM

Interviewee Name	**Location**
Assessor Name	**Date**

Project Name

What do you like about the way the new system operates?

What don't you like about the way the new system operates?

Now that the system has been in place for a while, I think

The help line is easy to contact:	Yes ☐	n/a ☐	No ☐
Most of my problems are quickly solved by the help line:	Yes ☐	n/a ☐	No ☐
When things go wrong, I quickly get help:	Yes ☐	n/a ☐	No ☐
I rarely need to use help documentation or on-line help:	Yes ☐	n/a ☐	No ☐
I can rely on the new system:	Yes ☐	n/a ☐	No ☐
The information stored on the system is secure:	Yes ☐	n/a ☐	No ☐
The system is easy to use:	Yes ☐	n/a ☐	No ☐
The system responds fast enough:	Yes ☐	n/a ☐	No ☐

NEW PROCESS REVIEW FORM

Interviewee Name	Location
Assessor Name	Date

Project Name

Describe the new procedure

What do you like about the new procedure?

What don't you like about the new procedure?

Now that the procedure has been in place for a while, I think

The benefits of the new procedure are clear:	Yes ☐	n/a ☐	No ☐
The new procedure directly affects me:	Yes ☐	n/a ☐	No ☐
My new role is now easier to carry out:	Yes ☐	n/a ☐	No ☐
The team I work with approves of the new procedure:	Yes ☐	n/a ☐	No ☐

PROBLEM IDENTIFICATION FORM

Interviewee Name	Location
Assessor Name	Date

Project Name

What problems did you encounter while the new system/procedure was being developed and how were they resolved?

Immediately after the new procedures were put in place I think

Most people were advised of the changes:	Yes ☐	n/a ☐	No ☐
I knew who to see if there were problems with the changes:	Yes ☐	n/a ☐	No ☐
The benefits of the new procedures were explained:	Yes ☐	n/a ☐	No ☐
The transition to the new procedures went smoothly:	Yes ☐	n/a ☐	No ☐

Immediately after the IT system was put in place I think

The help line was easy to contact:	Yes ☐	n/a ☐	No ☐
Most of my problems were quickly solved by the help line:	Yes ☐	n/a ☐	No ☐
When things went wrong, I quickly got help:	Yes ☐	n/a ☐	No ☐
I could rely on the new system:	Yes ☐	n/a ☐	No ☐
I was given sufficient training to use the new system:	Yes ☐	n/a ☐	No ☐

REQUEST FOR ADDITIONAL IMPROVEMENTS FORM

Requester Name	Location
Approved by Name	Date

Describe the change you want made to the new procedure or system

Why do you want to make this change?

How will this change help you to do your job better?

How will this change help the business?

Date scheduled:	Date completed:

ADDITIONAL NOTES FORM

Subject	Date

Notes

Index